POCKET
BEIJING

Christopher Pitts & Robert Isenberg

Contents

Top: Temples, Summer Palace (p124)
Bottom: Mutianyu section,
The Great Wall (p138)

Plan Your Trip................4

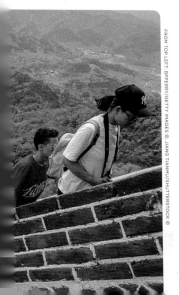

FROM TOP LEFT: BPPERRY/GETTY IMAGES ©; JIANG TIANMU/SHUTTERSTOCK ©

The Journey Begins Here

For many, Beijing is China. The centre of power since the 13th century, the city has seen successive dynasties come and go, from the Mongols to the Manchus to Mao. Each regime left its own indelible mark – the Forbidden City, Summer Palace, Tiananmen Square – and these reminders of a rich and storied past are what draw most visitors. But walking the streets amid glitzy new skyscrapers, straight-backed soldiers and thousands of made-in-China electric cars, it's impossible to miss another facet of the capital: the future. Self-confident and proud, timeless and yet constantly changing, Beijing never fails to surprise.

Christopher Pitts
christopherpitts.net
A lifelong admirer of Chinese art and calligraphy, Chris has written about China for twenty years. He is also the author of a forthcoming novel.

CONTRIBUTING WRITER
Robert Isenberg
robertisenberg.net
Robert is a writer and filmmaker based in Rhode Island. His most recent book is *Mile Markers: Essays on Cycling*.

Temple of Heaven (p73)
XIA YANG/GETTY IMAGES ©

THE BEST

Imperial Experiences

Home turf for the last three imperial dynasties, Beijing
is China's richest repository of historical attractions.
Most are aligned on the sacred central axis – the
centre of both the capital and the Chinese universe.

Discover the secretive world of 24
emperors and their thousands of
servants, from eunuchs to embroidery
maids, in the **Forbidden City**. (p38)

Climb the gravity-defying **Great Wall**,
the ultimate bucket-list adventure
that's draped dreamily across the
northern mountains (p132).

Delight in the esoteric symbolism
of the **Temple of Heaven**, where
emperors made sacrifices to
appease the gods. (p73)

Take in the temple-strewn gardens and
vast lake of the **Summer Palace**, the
favoured retreat of Cixi, the Empress
Dowager. (p124; pictured above left)

Learn everything about traditional
timekeeping at the **Drum and Bell
Towers**, which loom authoritatively
over the grey *hutong* rooftops. (p58)

Boat around **Beihai Park**, the former
imperial lake circled by Taoist temples
and crowned with a white Tibetan
stupa. (p84; pictured above right)

Right: Badaling section, Great Wall (p132)

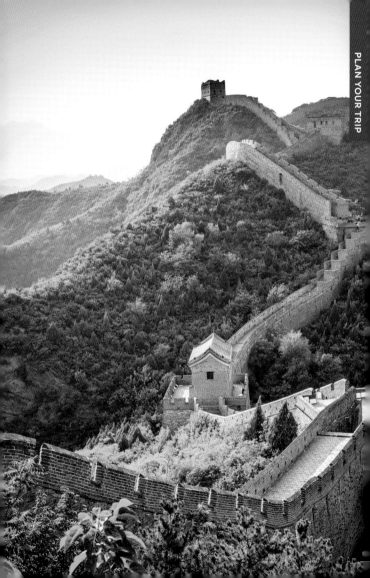

THE BEST

Shopping Experiences

Here a QR code, there a QR code...embrace the cashless economy as you snap up faux antiques, Buddhist prayer beads, traditional calligraphy, pearls, electronics and more.

Browse for faux antiques, arts and crafts and Communist-era kitsch at **Panjiayuan Market**, the emperor of Beijing's markets. (p110; pictured above)

Explore the alleyways of **Dashilar** and Liulichang Culture Street, filled with porcelain jewellery, art stores, antiques and booksellers. (p99)

Antique vase shards are turned into earrings, ornaments and boxes at the **Caicifang Porcelain Workshop**. (p99)

Sift through strings of freshwater pearls from Zhejiang at the **Hongqiao Pearl Market**, just outside the Temple of Heaven. (p78)

Sample traditional snacks like the doornail pie while browsing for fans, cloth slippers and silk along pedestrian **Qianmen Dajie**. (p77)

Treat yourself to a rare brick of *pǔ'ěr* tea or a prized Iron Guanyin oolong at **Maliandao Tea Market**. Tea sets, too. (p101; pictured above)

Right: Liulichang Culture Street (p99)

THE BEST

Temple Experiences

In imperial times, the capital was home to hundreds of temples and shrines, bringing in pilgrims and emissaries from across Asia. Marvel at the vestiges of Tibetan stupas, Taoist statuary, Khitan pagodas and the many altars of Confucian statecraft.

Make an offering at **Lama Temple**, historically one of the most important Tibetan lamaseries beyond the Himalayas' snowy peaks. (p60)

Step beneath the magnificent historic archways outside the peaceful **Confucius Temple & Imperial College**. (p65; pictured above)

Journey to the 76 departments of the Taoist underworld at **Dongyue Temple**, an island of medieval mysticism in Chaoyang. (p116; pictured above)

Admire the unique, India-inspired **Wuta Temple**, which dates to 1473 and has a fabulous stonemasonry museum. (p128)

Take in the magnificent sight of the 51m-high Tibetan stupa, the tallest in China, at **Miaoying Temple**. (p91)

Crane your neck and gaze at Beijing's oldest building, the 57.8m-tall, early-12th-century **Tianning Temple**. (p101)

Right: Miaoying Temple (p91)

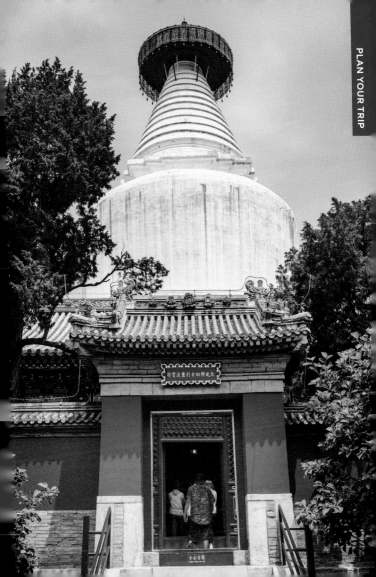

THE BEST

Museum Experiences

Beijing's historical vestiges and contemporary musings are displayed in museums and galleries across the city. From Han-dynasty figurines to transcendent statuary and court edicts to abstract expression, you'll find life in all its guises.

Visit the **National Museum of China**, a tour de force of art and artefacts from across Chinese history. (p36)

Distinguish the Khitan from the Han and the Mongols from the Manchu at the **Capital Museum**. (p90)

Pore over historical documents, imperial star charts, old maps and imperial edicts at the **First Historical Archives of China**. (p78)

See the best of Beijing's contemporary art at UCCA, one of the top galleries at the industrial **798 Art District**. (p112)

Follow Chinese emigration from Southeast Asia to the US at the excellent **Overseas Chinese History Museum**. (p65)

Put your finger on the pulse of contemporary Chinese art at the **National Art Museum**. (p46)

National Museum of China (p36)

TESTING/SHUTTERSTOCK ©

Best for Kids

Climb from watchtower to watchtower or slide down a toboggan at the **Great Wall**, an adventure like no other. (p132)

Hop on board your broomstick at Harry Potter and the Forbidden Journey, one of the many thrilling rides at **Universal Beijing Resort**. (p140)

Get out on the lakes at **Beihai Park**, whether in a boat in the summer or on skates and ice trikes in the winter. (p84)

Explore the maze of rooms and passageways at the **Forbidden City**, where little emperors have all the space in the world to let off some steam. (p38)

Best for Free

Stand beneath the watchful gaze of Mao at **Tiananmen Square**, Beijing's most politically charged public space. (p34)

Discover millennia of history, from Shang dynasty bronzes to priceless porcelain, at the showpiece **National Museum of China**. (p36)

Ferret out the beguiling temple complex prosaically known as the **Workers' Cultural Palace**, Beijing's best-kept secret. It's right beside the Forbidden City and is as good as free at just ¥2. (p44)

Get clued up on Beijing's storied history at the architecturally gorgeous **Capital Museum**. (p90)

Unravel the story of a historic *hutong* in central Beijing at the **Shijia Hutong Museum**, which provides access to a traditional courtyard home. (p48)

Admire the courage and impact of China's worldwide diaspora at the **Overseas Chinese History Museum**. (p65)

Three Perfect Days

From the Great Wall to the Forbidden City to roast duck, Beijing has a number of bucket-list experiences. Here are some ways to fit them all into a single action-packed schedule.

Revolutionary statues, Tiananmen Square (p34)

DAY ONE

Only Have One Day?

MORNING

Where else to begin but at the the very heart of the Chinese universe. Enter **Tiananmen Square** (p34) to grab a photo of the iconic Mao portrait (arrive at dawn for the flag-raising ceremony) before passing beneath his gaze to explore the byzantine world of the **Forbidden City** (p38; pictured above).

AFTERNOON

After lunch at the **Icehouse** (p39), continue your tour of the Forbidden City before exiting at the rear gate. Climb to the top of **Jingshan Park** (p45), which provides imperial views over all Beijing.

EVENING

Grab a cab to **Sìjì Mínfú** (p51) and join the queues for some of the best roast duck in the capital.

DAY TWO

A Weekend Trip

MORNING

Rise and shine, hikers! You're headed for a Great Wall (pictured above) adventure at either **Badaling** (p132; accessible by bullet train, one hour) or **Mutianyu** (p138; take the tourist bus, 90 minutes). Scramble steep watchtowers and snap photos of the Wall snaking over the hills. If you're after a wilder section of wall, consider an organised hiking tour.

AFTERNOON

Back in the city, recharge over a hotpot feast or spicy Sichuan crayfish at the raucous late-night eateries along **Ghost St** (p66) or try out the legions of trendy restaurants in **Sanlitun** (p118).

EVENING

For DJs stay in **Chaoyang** (p116); for live music head to the bars near the Drum Tower, like **Modernista** (p69).

DAY THREE

A Short Break

MORNING

Observe Beijingers dancing and performing taichi as you roam the **Temple of Heaven** (p73; pictured above), before admiring its grand centrepiece, the Hall of Prayer for Good Harvests. Pop into the **Pearl Market** (p78) by the park's east gate for souvenirs.

AFTERNOON

Make like the empress dowager and leave the city for the serenity of the **Summer Palace** (p124), out towards Beijing's Western Hills. Climb Longevity Hill for the grand view, then boat across Kunming Lake.

EVENING

Return to Beijing and head to the modern Qianliang Hutong for hip noodle joint **Pang Mei Noodles** (p51), followed by craft beer at **Jing-A Longfusi** (p53).

If You Have More Time

Make a beeline for the incomparable **Lama Temple** (p60) and its 18m-tall sandalwood Buddha. From here it's a short stroll to the comparatively quiet grounds of the **Confucius Temple** (p65). Follow the temple tour with a bike ride through the *hutong* to the **Drum Tower** (p58), at the northern end of the central axis.

Stroll around Houhai Lake, with a stop at **Song Qingling's Former Residence** (p87), or climb to the top of Jade Islet in **Beihai Park** (p84), crowned with a white Tibetan stupa. Alternatively, the Tibetan stupa at **Miaoying Temple** (p91) is even grander, tucked away amid the *hutong* in Xicheng.

If you're all templed out, head to the **Panjiayuan Market** (p110) where you can haggle your heart out for that one-of-a-kind souvenir: genuine copies of the Little Red Book, traditional ink and brush artwork, hand-carved chops and plenty of faux antiques. Finish the day with a Peking opera performance at the historic **Zhengyici Theatre** (p102).

Drum Tower (p58)

A City Day Trip

Judging by the size of the queues, the capital's most popular sight is neither the Great Wall nor the Forbidden City: it's **Universal Beijing Resort** (p140). A hop, skip and a metro ride east of the city centre, the theme park has brought a liberal sprinkle of Hollywood glitter to the Middle Kingdom.
If you plan on making the trip here to see the crooked chimneys and quaint rooftops of Hogsmeade, definitely count on staying for the entire day. Jurassic World Adventure (pictured above) and Kung Fu Panda are just some of the other themed lands, and the scream-worthy 3D rides and Instagrammable Potterland photo ops can be found around every corner.

On a Rainy Day

Don't be fooled by the Soviet-style exterior of the monolithic **National Museum of China** (p36), this is Beijing's best all-in-one museum, ranging from historical artefacts to Buddhist statuary to socialist-realism propaganda.

At the other end of the spectrum is the tiny **Poly Art Museum** (p50) – just two rooms, but fabulously curated. For contemporary expression, take a trip out to the **798 Art District** (p112; pictured above), a collection of edgy galleries in an industrial setting.

The **Overseas Chinese History Museum** (p65) is worth a trip, as is the **First Historical Archives of China** (p78), opened in 2022. Meanwhile, woodworkers and architecture aficionados should check out the oft-overlooked **Ancient Architecture Museum** (p102).

17

Get Prepared

Manners Matter

Generally speaking, China is very relaxed when it comes to etiquette. The most important thing to remember is to not make people lose face in public (eg by arguing or losing your cool).

Greetings and goodbyes Shake hands. Say *nǐ hǎo* to greet someone, and *zàijiàn* to say goodbye.

WeChat If a stranger asks to add you as a friend in a public setting, it's good form to accept.

WeChat

WeChat (微信; Wēixìn) is the single most useful app in China. It's social networking, texting, cashless payment and the internet all rolled into one. In order to reserve or purchase admission tickets, visitors need to use WeChat. You'll need to add: (1) a credit or debit card (add them at home; include a backup) and (2) a phone number and data plan that's active in China (buy at the airport).

Things to Know

Alipay (支付宝; Zhīfùbǎo) Few people in China use cash (though it is accepted). The Alipay app makes riding the metro, hailing a taxi and transferring money a breeze. Add your cards at home.

Local Phone Number In order to do most things in China, you need two things: (1) a local phone number and (2) your passport. While you can get around without a phone number, life will be much simpler if you buy a local SIM card at the airport. You must carry your passport with you at all times.

Limits Alipay and WeChat have transaction limits (¥3000) and charge a 3% fee for transfers/purchases over ¥200.

Intranet The World Wide Web has little presence in China. Only rarely will you find practical information or ticket-booking services online. In its place is WeChat, which only accesses China-based (and Chinese-language) data.

VPN & Maps

In order to bypass the Great Firewall and connect with the outside world (via Google, Gmail, Instagram, WhatsApp etc), you will need a VPN.

Research the latest on Reddit (r/chinalife) – what works changes constantly – and activate the plan before entering China. Have a backup and do not expect a seamless 100% success rate.

In terms of getting around, Apple Maps is the most reliable (no VPN needed), though it's not up to date. If you can read Chinese, Baidu Maps is current, though it's not particularly user-friendly.

DAILY BUDGET

BUDGET Less than ¥700

- Budget hotel: ¥300–400
- Lunch and dinner in local restaurants: ¥40–100
- Local beer: ¥10
- Subway fare: ¥3–20

MIDRANGE ¥700–1500

- Double room in a hotel: ¥600–1000
- Lunch and dinner in midrange restaurants: ¥100–400
- Taxi trips: ¥50
- Admission to main sights: ¥50–150

TOP END More than ¥1500

- Double room in a luxury hotel: from ¥1200
- Dinner at a stylish restaurant: ¥250–500
- Drinks at cocktail bars: ¥80–130
- Guided tour: ¥200–1000

Currency
Yuan (¥; 元)

Language
Mandarin

Time
China Standard Time (GMT/ UTC plus eight hours)

TIP

Use a translation app like DeepL or Baidu Translate to act as your personal interpreter. These apps work by taking a picture (eg of a museum caption or a menu) or by speaking into your phone.

KAMIL ZAJACZKOWSKI/SHUTTERSTOCK ©

When To Go

Beijing is most pleasant in spring (April and May) and autumn (September and October), though avoid the week after National Day (1 October).

Beijing's seasons each have their own peculiarities. Spring can be lovely, but watch out for dust storms that blow in from the Gobi Desert in March and early April. Summers are hot and humid, but the heat is tempered by frequent rainstorms. Autumn brings clear skies and pleasant temperatures, and is ideal for exploring the Great Wall. Winter is cold and dark, with bitter winds that sweep down from the steppe. On the plus side, sub-zero temperatures in January and February bring opportunities to ice skate at public lakes around town.

Traditional Festivals

January or February Kicking off on Chinese New Year's Eve and lasting for 15 days, the family-oriented **Spring Festival** (春节; Chūn Jié) is China's most important holiday. Beijing will be quieter than usual at first as most people are at home celebrating; however, all the big sights should be open. Look out for temple fairs (庙会; miàohuì) during this time.

4 or 5 April Tomb Sweeping Day (清明节; Qīngmíng Jié) is a day set aside for ancestor worship. You may see residents burning ghost money for their dearly departed, although recently the government has clamped down on this practice.

May or June The fifth day of the fifth lunar month marks the **Dragon Boat Festival** (端午节; Duānwǔ Jié), when Chinese eat zòngzi (sticky rice wrapped in bamboo leaves) and dragon-boat races are occasionally staged on Beijing's lakes.

Beijing Weather

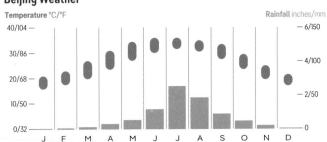

Temperature °C/°F — Rainfall inches/mm

Temple Fair, Spring Festival, Ditan Park (p67)

September or October Also known as the Moon Festival, the **Mid-Autumn Festival** (中秋节; Zhōngqiū Jié) is marked by eating *yuèbǐng* (mooncakes) and celebrating family reunions.

Other Events

January or February Celebrated on the 15th day of Spring Festival, **Lantern Festival** (元宵节; Yuánxiāo Jié) is known for its delicious *yuánxiāo* (glutinous rice dumplings).

1 May May Day (五一; Wǔyī), or International Workers' Day, kicks off a five-day national holiday, when tourist sites are jam-packed.

Hotel availability plummets; avoid if possible.

August A citywide celebration of classical music, the **Beijing Music Festival** (北京国际音乐节; Beijing Guójì Yīnyuè Jié; bmf.org. cn) brings together performers at venues around town.

1 October National Day (国庆节; Guóqìng Jié) marks the anniversary of the founding of the PRC. There are huge military parades on key years, and it kicks off **Golden Week**, a seven-day national holiday that sees tourist sights full to bursting. Avoid travelling during this week if possible.

ACCOMMODATION LOWDOWN

Accommodation is hardest to find during the big Chinese holidays, in particular the weeks of 1 May and 1 October, when the entire nation has time off and millions of people are travelling. In contrast, cheap periods include Christmas, January and the post-Chinese New Year lull.

Getting There

Beijing can be reached by plane, train, bus or a combination of ship and train, but most overseas travellers fly into the city, arriving at Beijing Capital International Airport (PEK) or Beijing Daxing International Airport (PKX).

From the Airport

Beijing Capital International Airport

Airport Express The Airport Express train (¥25, 30 minutes, 6.21am to 11.10pm) links terminals 2 and 3 with central Beijing at Dongzhimen subway station, with transfers to lines 2, 10 and 13.

Taxis Taxis are relatively cheap (around ¥90 to ¥140) and take 30 minutes to one hour, depending on your destination and traffic. Use the official taxi rank only.

Bus There are a dozen airport shuttles to destinations in and around Beijing (¥20 to ¥30, around 70 minutes), including the main railway stations. However, the Airport Express is faster and more convenient.

Beijing Daxing International Airport

This massive airport serves Beijing, Tianjin and Hebei province.

Train & Metro The high-speed Beijing–Xiong'an Intercity Railway runs to the Beijing West Railway Station (¥30, 30 minutes, 6.40am to 8.56pm), where you can transfer to metro lines 7 and 9.

The more frequent Daxing metro currently only runs to Caoqiao station south of the city (¥35, 35 minutes, 6.30am to 10.30pm), where you can transfer to lines 10 and 19. This is still a long way from central Beijing.

Taxi Taxis into town cost about ¥220 and take 60 to 90 minutes to central Beijing. Use the official taxi rank only.

Other Points of Entry

Train

China's HSR (High-Speed Rail) train network is the longest and busiest in the world. Most journeys between other major cities and Beijing use G-category bullet trains that race along at over 300km/h.

Beijing has four major train stations for long-distance travel: Beijing, Beijing West, Beijing South and Beijing North. There are international routes to and from Mongolia, North Korea, Russia and Vietnam, and trains to and from Hong Kong and Lhasa in Tibet.

🚋 Getting Around

Beijing's extensive metro system, cheap taxi fares and ubiquitous shared bikes make getting around the city a breeze. However, you should still prepare for lots of walking as some of the big sights, such as the Forbidden City and Tiananmen Square, can only be accessed in an indirect fashion on foot.

Subway

The world's busiest and longest subway system, Beijing's metro has 27 lines (over 800km) burrowing through the municipality.

Exceedingly foreigner-friendly, all signs, announcements, maps and ticket machines are in English. It's cheap by world standards, too, with distance-based fares costing between ¥3 and ¥10.

To spot a subway station, look for the navy-blue sign with a white capital 'D' (for *dìtiě zhàn;* 地铁站; subway station) enclosed in a circle. You'll need to pass through security each time you ride the metro.

To plan a journey and get an idea of travel times, download the Explore Beijing metro app.

Taxi & Rideshares

Taxis (出租车; *chūzūchē*) are everywhere, but good luck hailing one during rush hour, in rainstorms and between 8pm and 10pm – prime time for the post-dinner homeward rush. It's easiest to hail a taxi online using DiDi or another app, but you must have a local phone number and payment app.

You can always flag one down the old-fashioned way if needed.

--- **ESSENTIAL APP** ---
Alipay does it all: use it to ride the subway, hail a cab, rent a bike and more. Scan the QR code above right for Apple. Scan the QR code below right for Android.

Flagfall is ¥13, and lasts for 3km. After that it's ¥2.3 per kilometre. Rates increase after 11pm.

It's very rare for drivers to speak any English, so always have the name and address of your destination written down in Chinese characters (not pinyin), and keep your hotel's business card on you to get back home again.

Bicycle

Cycling is the most enjoyable way to get around Beijing, especially in summer (p67). The city is as flat as a dumpling wrapper and almost every road has a wide bike lane.

Beijing also has thousands of shared bikes, which are incredibly convenient...if you have a local phone number, a linked payment card and are able to navigate the registration process.

At the time of writing, the light-blue Hello Bike (哈啰单车; Hāluō Dānchē) was the most convenient option for foreigners, as it included a translation feature within the Alipay mini-app and supported foreign passports as a form of ID.

Public Bus

Beijing's buses (公共汽车; gōnggòng qìchē) are plentiful and cheap (from ¥2 per journey), but because stops are indicated in Chinese only and routes are often circuitous, they can be tricky for tourists to use.

Public Transport Essentials

Digital Payments

Paying for transport in Beijing is cash-free and incredibly convenient, but you have to be able to register within the Chinese system and set up a recognised form of payment. If you're in town for only two or three days, you may find the process to be more trouble than it's worth.

Subway

Riding the metro is simple: open Alipay, select 'Transport' and then 'Metro'. Scan the QR code once to enter the station and again when you exit. The fare will be deducted automatically from your card.

Taxi & DiDi

Download the DiDi app in your home country. When you want to hail a cab, open DiDi (or the mini-app within WeChat or Alipay) and enter your destination. A selection of different vehicles will appear, along with the fare.

When your ride arrives, the driver may ask you (in Chinese) to confirm the last four digits of your phone number. Have the numbers handy and show them to the driver. Press 'pay' (支付; zhīfù) at the end of your ride.

You will need a local phone number to use DiDi.

Using Cash

Not everyone will be able or want to use their phone for payments. Cash is still accepted, just make sure you carry a variety of bills as few people will have exact change. ATMs are generally easy to find, though not all take foreign cards. Credit cards are usually only accepted at hotels and high-end businesses.

Subways

To ride the subway, you can either buy a single ticket at the automated machines or pick up a travel card (交通一卡通; *jiāotōng yīkǎtōng;* ¥20 deposit) at a subway-station info desk and load money onto it. A transport card means you won't need to buy a ticket each time you ride.

TRAVEL COSTS

Metro
from ¥3

Bike Share
per half-hour ¥1.5

Taxi
from ¥13

— **ID CHECKS** —

The police sometimes conduct random ID checks in the subway. Keep your passport handy.

TIPS FOR GETTING TRANSPORT APPS TO WORK

- Have a good photo of your passport preloaded on your phone. You will need to upload it to use various services.
- Upon arrival in China, buy a local SIM card at the airport – note that at the time of research, there was only one desk, and it was inconveniently located immediately upon exiting customs. Do not buy an eSIM in your home country, as these do not include a local phone number that's tied to your passport, which is essential.
- Note that Wise (wise.com) offers an electronic debit card. It does not charge transaction fees, and exchange rates are excellent, though your bank will likely charge you an initial wire fee to load money onto the card.

A Few Surprises

Amid all the 21st-century shopping malls and futuristic skyscrapers are remnants of an ancient city whose roots reach far into the past.

Hutong

The essence of Beijing is its *hutong* (胡同), the distinctive, grey-brick alleyways that criss-cross parts of the capital. These timeless residential lanes, where everyday life unfolds at a slower pace than elsewhere, offer a glimpse of traditional community life. Not so long ago, most of the inner city was a giant chessboard of *hutong* and courtyard homes, but today they only endure in scattered patches across the old centre. Take a *hutong* tour with **Beijing Postcards** (p100) or visit **Shijia Hutong Museum** (p49).

Sacrificial Sites

Beijing's collection of imperial altars and temples distinguishes it from other Chinese cities. The emperor and imperial court held sacrifices to protect the empire from divine catastrophe. The sacrificial sites included nine altars, such as the **Temple of Heaven** (p73) or the Temple of Agriculture, now the **Ancient Architecture Museum** (p102), and multiple ancestor temples, such as the **Workers' Cultural Palace** (p44), **Temple of Ancient Monarchs** (p91) and **Shouhuang Palace** (p45).

Modern Architecture

In 1997, the CCP announced a plan to triple the living space of Chinese city residents, usually by moving millions of people from their traditional homes (which often lacked amenities like plumbing) into planned satellite towns beyond the centre. Skyscrapers and shopping centres sprung up in their place in the two decades that followed – which earned China a reputation as an architect's playground – until President Xi issued a moratorium on 'weird' buildings in 2016. Gaze at some of Beijing's landmark designs from the 80th-floor bar **Atmosphere** (p116).

OFFBEAT BEIJING

Hidden between the Forbidden City and Tiananmen Square are two cypress-dotted parks: **Workers' Cultural Palace** (p44) and **Zhongshan Park** (p44).

Azimuths, sextants and the traditional calendar star at the capital's **Ancient Observatory** (p49).

Little-known **Guardian Art Center** (p47) holds exhibits of Chinese artisanship and international art.

See the only surviving remnants of the city walls at the **Southeast Corner Watchtower** (p77).

Shijia Hutong Museum (p48)

Zhongshan Park (p44)

Explore Beijing

Worth a Trip

Beijing's Walking Tours

Kunming Lake, Summer Palace (p125)
GONG HANGXU/GETTY IMAGES ©

See p51
for eating
and drinking
listings

Explore
Forbidden City & Dongcheng Central

Here, at the middle of the Middle Kingdom, is the Beijing you came to see: Chairman Mao slumbering in his mausoleum on Tiananmen Square and the ghosts of emperors past haunting the 9999 rooms of the world's largest palace complex, the Forbidden City. Remarkably, central Beijing retains its historic layout, a fantastical arrangement of divine order. You'll understand as soon as you clamber up the slopes of Jingshan Park and drink in the astonishing scale and symmetry of the city's central axis from above. Get off the beaten path with a trip to the lesser-known temples and museums in the surrounding *hutong*.

Getting Around

Ⓢ **Subway Line 1**
Runs east–west; stops at Tiananmen East (Tiananmen Square and the Forbidden City), Wangfujing (food courts) and Jiangguomen (Ancient Observatory).

Ⓢ **Subway Line 2**
Runs in a circle; stops at Qianmen (Tiananmen Square), Jiangguomen (Ancient Observatory) and Dongsi Shitiao (Poly Art Museum).

Ⓢ **Subway Line 5**
Runs north–south; stops at Dengshikou (Shijia Hutong Museum) and Zhangzizhong Lu (restaurants).

Ⓢ **Subway Line 8**
Runs north–south; stops at Jinyu Hutong (Forbidden City) and the National Art Museum.

Doorway, the Forbidden City (p38)
BEN COX/SHUTTERSTOCK ©

THE BEST

HISTORIC SIGHT
Forbidden City (p38)

COMMUNIST LANDMARK
Tiananmen Square (p34)

PEKING DUCK
Sìjì Mínfú (p51)

PANORAMIC VIEWS
Jingshan Park (p45)

ARTWORK
National Museum of China (p36)

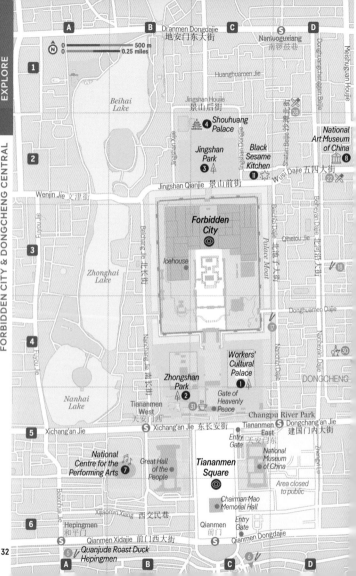

Di'anmen Dongdajie
地安门东大街

Nanluoguxiang
南锣鼓巷

Huangchenggengen Beijie

Meishuguan Houjie

Beihai
Lake

Jingshan Houjie
景山后街

Shouhuang **4**
Palace

National
Art Museum
of China **8**

Jingshan
Park **3**

Black
Sesame
Kitchen **11**

Wusi Dajie 五四大街

Jingshan Qianjie 景山前街

Wenjin Jie 文津街

Forbidden
City

Icehouse

Zhonghai
Lake

Palace Moat

Qihetou Jie

Donghuamen Dajie

Zhongshan
Park **2**

Workers'
Cultural
Palace **1**

DONGCHENG

Nanhai
Lake

Tiananmen
West
天安门西

Gate of
Heavenly
Peace **31**

Changpu River Park

Xichang'an Jie

Xichang'an Jie 东长安街

Tiananmen
East 天安门东

Dongchang'an Jie
建国门内大街

National
Centre for the
Performing Arts **7**

Great Hall
of the
People

Tiananmen
Square

Entry
Gate

National
Museum
of China

Area closed
to public

Chairman Mao
Memorial Hall

Hepingmen
和平门

Xijiaomin Xiang 西交民巷

Entry
Gate

Qianmen Xidajie 前门西大街

Qianmen
前门

Qianmen Dongdajie

Quanjude Roast Duck **5**
Hepingmen

E Zhangzizhonglu
张自忠路

S Dongsishitiao Lu **F** Dongsi Batiao 东四八条

G

Dongsi Shitiao **S** **H**
东四十条

Poly Art 16
Museum 🏛

Chaoyangmen Beidajie

1

Dongsi Liutiao 东四六条 20

24

Qiantang Hutong 23

National
Art Museum
中国美术馆

Dongsi Beidajie 东四北大街

9 Guardian 东四西大街
Art Center

Dongsi Xidajie **S** Chaoyangmennei Dajie

Dongsi
东四

Chaoyangmen **S**
朝阳门

2

Dongerhuan (East 2nd Ring Rd) 二环

Baofang Hutong

Baofang Hutong

Wangfujing Dajie 王府井大街

Dongsi Nandajie 东四南大街

Yanyue Hutong
演乐胡同

Neiwubu Jie
Shijia Hutong

Dafangjia Hutong

3

Dengshikou Xijie 灯市口西街

13 Slow
Lane

Zhihua 🏛
Temple 15

S Jinyu Hutong
金鱼胡同
27
21

Shijia Hutong 12
Museum 🏛

Ganmian
Hutong

Lumicang Hutong 禄米仓胡同

Jinyu Hutong
金鱼胡同

Dengshikou
灯市口 **S**

Jinbao Jie

Jinbao Jie

Yabao Lu

29

19

Wangfujing Dajie 王府井大街

10 Wangfujing
Street

Dongdan Beidajie 东单北大街

Dongcang Nanxiaojie

Dongzongbu Hutong 东总部胡同

4

Dongerhuan (East 2nd Ring Rd) 二环

26

Dongdan Santiao

25 Oriental
Plaza

Jianguomen **S**
建国门

Dongchang'an Jie
Wangfujing **S**
王府井 东长安街

Dongdan
东单

Jianguomennei Dajie
建国门内大街

S

14
Ancient
Observatory

5

Taijichang
Toutiao

Taijichang Dajie 台基厂大街

Dongdan
Park

Chongwenmennei Dajie

Beijingzhan Jie

Dongjiaomin Xiang 东交民巷

Chongwenmen Xidajie

S Chongwenmen
崇文门

Chongwenmen Dongdajie
崇文门东大街

Beijingzhan Dongjie

For more see

Top Experiences ⭐ p34
Experiences ⭐ p44
Eating ✕ p51
Drinking ◉ p53

6

E **F** **G** **H**

33

Tiananmen Square

Flanked by triumphalist Soviet-style buildings, Tiananmen Square (天安门广场, Tiān'ānmén Guǎngchǎng) is hallowed ground for the Communist Party. Watched over by Mao's portrait and haunted by the protesters of generations past, it's not the most easy-going of places, but it remains one of the nation's most stirring destinations.

MAP P32 **C5**

PLANNING TIP
Advance reservations must be made via WeChat. You'll need to ask a local travel agent or your concierge to arrange this unless you can read Chinese and have a local phone number.

Scan to reserve a ticket for Tiananmen Square through a local travel agent

Entrance & Orientation

At the time of writing, Tiananmen had two main entrances: one at the Tiananmen East subway stop (line 1) and the other at the Qianmen subway stop (line 2). Security is tight: your bags will be checked at least once, and you will be asked to show your passport multiple times (reservations are tied to your passport number, so you don't need a digital ticket). Queues in the morning can easily last up to two hours, but are often shorter in the afternoon. When you gain access to the square, you'll be able to visit three other sights: the Chairman Mao Memorial Hall (in the centre), the National Museum of China (east) and the Gate of Heavenly Peace (north). If you are planning on visiting the Forbidden City on the same day, visit Tiananmen first, as you cannot enter the square in the reverse direction.

The Square

The rectangular arrangement of Tiananmen Square, its many red flags rippling in the wind, to some extent pays obeisance to traditional Chinese culture, but most of its ornaments and buildings are Soviet-inspired. Mao conceived the square to project the power of the Communist Party, and during the Cultural Revolution he reviewed

Soldiers, the Gate of Heavenly Peace (p36)
CHAMELEONSEYE/SHUTTERSTOCK ©

parades of up to a million people here. In the centre of the square is the Monument to the People's Heroes, a 40m-tall obelisk.

Prior to the fall of the Qing dynasty, this area was home to the imperial court's most important ministries, which flanked a long walkway leading from the Inner City walls and Qianmen Gate (currently off-limits) at the square's southern end. It has also traditionally been the site where commoners and officials could publicly lodge grievances with the emperor. This practice was revived several times over the course of the 20th century, initially on 4 May 1919 (when students called for a stronger government), and most tragically in 1989, following the death of the reform-minded general secretary Hu Yaobang, when disgruntled students and workers again protested against authorities.

QUICK BREAK
A few simple cafeterias are located in the square's southeastern corner, near the Qianmen entrance. If you have tickets for the National Museum, its cafe is better.

1989 PROTESTS
Tiananmen Square is best known outside China for the tragic events of 3–4 June 1989. After six weeks of pro-democracy protests, when up to a million students and workers occupied the square, the army was sent in to crush the 'counter-revolutionary riot'. Few young people in China today know anything about the protests and subsequent deaths, a black mark that has been scrubbed from the collective conscience.

Early risers can watch the daily sunrise **flag-raising ceremony**, performed by a troop of People's Liberation Army (PLA) soldiers marching at precisely 108 paces per minute, 75cm per pace. The reverse ceremony is at sunset.

Chairman Mao Memorial Hall

One of Beijing's more surreal spectacles is the sight of Mao Zedong's embalmed corpse on public display in his **mausoleum** (毛主席纪念堂, Máo Zhǔxí Jìniàntáng), located at the heart of Tiananmen Square. You must make advance reservations via WeChat (Chinese only); it's open 8am to noon, Tuesday to Sunday. Tickets are hard to get.

National Museum of China

Beijing's best **museum** (中国国家博物馆, Zhōngguó Guójiā Bówùguǎn) is unfortunately ensconced within the massive Tiananmen security zone, meaning you'll need to pass through security queues twice (once for the square and again for the museum) to get in. Despite the hurdles, it is absolutely worth it. The basement is the star attraction, where numerous galleries introduce artefacts that span the entirety of Chinese civilisation, from prehistoric jade and bronze pieces through Han dynasty figurines, and on to priceless ceramics, calligraphy and Buddhist sculptures. The building, a socialist-realist block, is east of the square and was one of Mao's Ten Great Buildings erected in 1959 to celebrate a decade of the PRC. Separate advance reservations are required (via WeChat, in Chinese).

Gate of Heavenly Peace

Instantly recognisable by its giant framed portrait of Mao, the double-eaved **Gate of Heavenly Peace** (天安门, Tiān'ānmén) is a potent national symbol. Formerly the largest of the four gates of the Imperial City Wall, it was from here that Mao proclaimed the founding of the People's Republic

Chairman Mao Memorial Hall
RICHIE CHAN/SHUTTERSTOCK ©

of China in 1949, and where every president since has addressed the nation and surveyed military parades. The gate has incredible views of the square and absolutely merits a climb, but you need advance tickets (via WeChat, in Chinese), which sell out quickly. Foreigners must first show their passport at the customer service window, pick up a paper ticket and then check all bags before entering. The balcony is about as sacred a space as you can find in communist China, so be on your best behaviour.

Even if you don't have tickets, you can still walk beneath the gate, which takes you to the Forbidden City. Visit this sight last: once you pass beneath it, you cannot turn around to re-enter Tiananmen Square.

GREAT HALL OF THE PEOPLE
Monolithic and intimidating, the Stalinist Great Hall of the People (1959) west of Tiananmen Square houses the highest organ of state power, the National People's Congress (NPC). It was closed to foreigners at the time of writing.

EXPLORE

FORBIDDEN CITY & DONGCHENG CENTRAL

Forbidden City

For all its antiquity, only a century has passed since the last emperor left the Forbidden City (紫禁城, Zǐjìn Chéng), the divine stronghold around which Beijing ripples outwards. On display within are all the treasures and tragedies of 24 rulers and their consorts, eunuchs and palace maids.

MAP P32 **C3**

PLANNING TIP
Tickets must be reserved online and generally sell out far in advance. Try the 'ticket grabbing' service on the official website if the regular reservations are booked out.

Scan to reserve a ticket to the Forbidden City

Planning Your Visit

Although you can explore the Forbidden City in a few hours, a full day will keep you occupied – it is a truly colossal place. Much like the Louvre, you can't see it all at once, so focus on the parts that sound most interesting. Many visitors get caught up with the vast ceremonial halls and parade grounds of the **Outer Court** (southern half), but remember that the real thrill comes from exploring the **Inner Court**: the labyrinth of courtyards and halls north of the Outer Court, laid out on a more human scale.

If you are coming from Tiananmen Square, you'll enter via the **Gate of Heavenly Peace** (p36). Otherwise, the entrance is via the east side of the palace on **Donghuamen Dajie**, from where you'll cross the moat and follow it to the Meridian Gate.

After you pass through security, you can pick up an audio tour (¥40) before entering via the Meridian Gate. Note that the Forbidden City is closed on Mondays. Be prepared to walk long distances.

History

This gargantuan palace complex was built on the site of a palace dating to Kublai Khan and sheltered two dynasties of emperors (the Ming and the Qing). It may look decadent, but

Meridian Gate
DIGITAL FRIENDS/SHUTTERSTOCK ©

a stultifying code of rules and strict protocol – including a 4am to 8pm workday and the detailed documentation of the emperor's sex life – made life extremely regimented for rulers. In some sense, it was as if they were under a very lavish house arrest. And, in fact, during the Qing dynasty, many emperors preferred to escape the palace for the gardens of the **Old Summer Palace** (p129). It wasn't until 1911 that revolution came knocking at the huge doors, bringing with it the last orders for dynastic rule.

The Forbidden City was redubbed the Palace Museum (故宫博物馆, Gùgōng Bówùguǎn), and entry for the common people no longer meant instant death. It opened as a museum in 1925, just one year after Puyi, the abdicated last emperor, departed the Inner Court. The Forbidden City celebrated its 600th anniversary in 2020, and its 100th anniversary as a museum in 2025.

TAKE A BREAK
The coolest place to eat is beneath the vaulted ceilings of the former Icehouse (冰窖餐厅, Bīngjiào Cāntīng) west of the Gate of Heavenly Purity. Don't confuse it with the similarly named cafe.

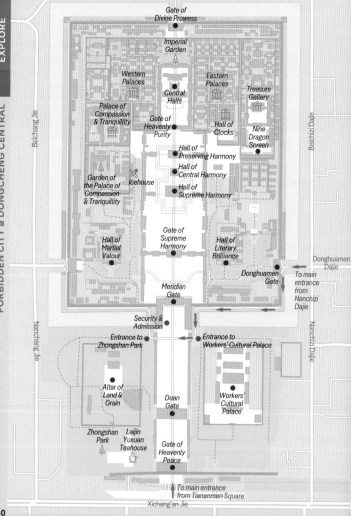

FORBIDDEN CITY & DONGCHENG CENTRAL

Jingshan Qianjie

Gate of
Divine Prowess

Imperial
Garden

Western
Palaces

Eastern
Palaces

Treasure
Gallery

Central
Halls

Palace of
Compassion
& Tranquillity

Gate of
Heavenly
Purity

Hall of
Clocks

Nine
Dragon
Screen

Beichang Jie

Beichizi Dajie

Hall of
Preserving
Harmony

Hall of
Central Harmony

Garden of
the Palace of
Compassion
& Tranquillity

Icehouse

Hall of
Supreme Harmony

Hall of
Martial
Valour

Gate of
Supreme
Harmony

Hall of
Literary
Brilliance

Donghuamen
Dajie

Donghuamen
Gate

Meridian
Gate

To main
entrance
from
Nanchizi
Dajie

Security &
Admission

Entrance to
Zhongshan Park

Entrance to
Workers' Cultural Palace

Nanchang Jie

Nanchizi Dajie

Altar of
Land &
Grain

Workers'
Cultural
Palace

Duan
Gate

Zhongshan
Park

Laijin
Yuxuan
Teahouse

Gate of
Heavenly Peace

To main entrance
from Tiananmen Square

Xichang'an Jie

Outer Court

The Outer Court is dominated by the Three Great Halls set in vast cobbled courtyards, which could hold thousands of dignitaries and their sedan chair bearers, guards and servants.

The **Hall of Supreme Harmony** is the most important and largest structure in the Forbidden City. It was used for state occasions, such as the emperor's birthday, coronations and the nomination of military leaders. Inside the Hall of Supreme Harmony is a richly decorated Dragon Throne, from which the emperor would preside over trembling officials. Behind the Hall of Supreme Harmony is the square **Hall of Central Harmony**, which was used as the emperor's transit lounge. Here he would make last-minute preparations, rehearse speeches and receive ministers. The third of the Great Halls is the **Hall of Preserving Harmony**, used for banquets and later for the palace examinations.

Side Galleries

The Outer Court's side galleries make for peaceful detours: the **Hall of Martial Valour** is where emperors received ministers. The **Hall of Literary Brilliance** complex was formerly used as a residence by the crown prince. Both house rotating exhibitions.

Inner Court

Unless you have all day, focus on just one or two sections within the Inner Court. All are fascinating.

Palace of Compassion & Tranquillity

West of the Hall of Preserving Harmony is the **Palace of Compassion & Tranquillity** (1536), where the empresses and consorts of deceased emperors resided, not being permitted to serve the new emperor. The main complex has an excellent exhibit of Buddhist statuary, while the adjacent **Palace of Longevity & Health** unveils the period furnishings of the Empress Dowager Chongqing (1736–77). Directly south is the **Garden of the Palace of Compassion & Tranquillity**.

YANXI PALACE
It's hard to get a sense of what life inside the Forbidden City was actually like on a visit, but for a dramatic reimagining, watch *Yanxi Palace*, a lush (albeit somewhat silly) television drama that follows the quick-witted embroidery maid Wei Yingluo as she navigates the perils of court life and rises to power among the imperial consorts. Bertolucci's gorgeous *The Last Emperor*, meanwhile, was filmed on site.

IMPERIAL GARDEN

At the northern end of the Forbidden City is the Imperial Garden, where emperors and their consorts could retreat to read, relax, sip tea and stroll past rockeries and ancient cypresses. At its centre is the double-eaved Hall of Imperial Peace. The Lodge of Spiritual Cultivation is where Scottish tutor Sir Reginald Johnston gave English lessons to the abdicated emperor Puyi.

Treasure Gallery

East of the Hall of Preserving Harmony is the extensive **Palace of Tranquil Longevity**, also known as the Treasure Gallery (separate ¥10 admission), which the Qianlong Emperor built for his retirement (which he never took) in 1771. Today it comprises a number of atmospheric halls, gardens and courtyard buildings that hold some fine exhibits from the Palace Museum collection.

Highlights include the beautiful glazed **Nine Dragon Screen**, one of only three of its type left in China, and the Belvedere of Cheerful Melodies, a three-storey wooden opera house.

Before a visit to the Treasure Gallery, be sure to visit the **Hall of Clocks** and the **Hall of Abstinence**, where the emperor would purify himself before important rituals.

The Central Halls

The basic configuration of the Outer Court is echoed by the next group of buildings along the central axis, reached through the Gate of Heavenly Purity. Though smaller in scale, these buildings were more important in terms of real power, which in China traditionally lies at the back door.

The first structure is the **Palace of Heavenly Purity**, a residence of Ming and early Qing emperors, and later an audience hall for receiving foreign envoys and high officials. Immediately behind it is the **Hall of Union**, which contains a clepsydra – a water clock made in 1745 with five bronze vessels and a calibrated scale. The **Palace of Earthly Tranquillity** was the imperial couple's bridal chamber and where the empress ruled the Inner Court.

Eastern & Western Palaces

A dozen smaller palace courtyards lie east and west of the three lesser central halls. It was in these self-contained abodes where most emperors actually lived. Many of the buildings, particularly those to the west, are decked out in imperial furniture.

Nine Dragon Screen
ZHAO JIAN KANG/SHUTTERSTOCK ©

The six **eastern palaces** were the living quarters of imperial consorts and their sons during Qing times. Exhibitions here display a variety of cultural relics, from ceramics and jade to musical instruments and ceremonial bronze vessels. The most unusual is the Palace of Prolonging Happiness (aka Yanxi Palace), which features an unfinished 20th-century western-style building with an intricately carved white marble facade.

The six **western palaces** include the Palace of Gathered Elegance, which contains photographs and artefacts relating to the last emperor, Puyi, who lived here as a child ruler. The Palace of Earthly Honour, with its period interiors, was where Empress Dowager Cixi received courtiers on her 50th birthday. As a young consort, she lived in the Palace of Gathered Elegance to the north. At the head of the western palaces is the Hall of Mental Cultivation, often the emperor's residence and office.

THE CENTRAL AXIS
The Forbidden City is laid out almost symmetrically on a 7.8km north–south axis that extended south to Yongding Gate and north to the Drum and Bell Towers.

EXPERIENCES

From Ancestor
Worship to Class Struggle   PARK

MAP: **①** P32 **C4**

Hidden between Tiananmen
Square and the Forbidden City
are two havens of shaded park
space: the **Workers' Cultural
Palace** (劳动人民文化宫, Láodòng
Rénmín Wénhuà Gōng) to the east
and Zhongshan Park to the west.
Both are accessible to the public
without advance reservations for
either of the main sights.

For several centuries, the
Cultural Palace – originally known
as **Imperial Ancestral Temple**
(太庙, Tài Miào) – was one of the
most sacred temples in Beijing,
where emperors would come to
worship. Its three halls remain
an excellent example of Ming
architecture. Ancient cypress
and pine trees, one reputedly
planted by a Ming emperor, line
the approach to the Five-Coloured
Glazed Gate, said to be a 15th-
century original, which would
make it older than those in the
mostly Qing-era Forbidden City
next door.

Inside, marble bridges lead to
three flights of steps ascending
to the magnificent Sacrificial
Hall, which resembles the Hall
of Supreme Harmony in the
Forbidden City. Spirits alone
were permitted to traverse the
central plinth; the emperor
was consigned to the left-hand
flight. This hall would have held
the thrones of departed royals
and their consorts; now it holds
rotating calligraphy displays.

Sip Tea in Zhongshan Park   PARK

MAP: **②** P32 **B5**

Named after China's first
president Sun Yatsen (aka Sun
Zhongshan), whose body was
placed here briefly after his
death, this lovely park (中山公园,
Zhōngshān Gōngyuán) sits at
the southwest corner of the
Forbidden City. The park used
to be royal gardens containing
the sacred **Altar of Land &
Grain**, where the emperor
offered sacrifices twice a year.
The altar, a square open-air
dais, is the centrepiece; the
surrounding halls contain
displays on the sacrificial rituals.
In 1914, it became the first public
park in Beijing.

The real highlight here,
however, is the historic Laijin
Yuxuan Teahouse (p53), which
makes for an excellent place to
take a break in between visits
to Tiananmen Square and the
Forbidden City. Savour a cup
of jasmine tea and sample the
famous steamed buns (pork
and mustard greens), while the
soothing sounds of the Chinese
zither wash away the nearby
tourist hubbub. After it first
opened in 1915, it became a
popular meeting spot for Chinese
intellectuals, such as the writer
Lu Xun.

Climb to the Top of Jingshan Park

PARK

MAP: ❸ P32 C2

Beijing's finest park (景山公园, Jĭngshān Gōngyuán) is located directly across the road from the Forbidden City's north gate (the exit). At first glance, you would never guess that this is an artificial hill, but it was created centuries ago from the sediment excavated to make the palace moat. Its location is in accordance with feng shui principles, as it protects the palace from the negative yin energy – and dust storms – of the north.

A fitting coda to any Forbidden City tour, if you have the energy, is to clamber up to the 46m-high summit, which affords princely views of all Beijing and the palace below. Time your ascent for sunset and you'll have a knockout post on Instagram. Alternatively, visit in the early morning to join in with elderly folk going about their dawn routines of dancing, performing taichi or playing *jiànzi* (kick-shuttlecock).

On the park's eastern side, a Chinese scholar tree stands in the place where, according to legend, the last Ming emperor hanged himself as a peasant rebellion swarmed into the capital unopposed.

Imperial Veneration at Shouhuang Palace

TEMPLE

MAP: ❹ P32 C2

At the northern edge of Jingshan Park is **Shouhuang Palace** (寿皇

THE MANCHU

The Manchu were the rulers of China's last imperial dynasty, the Qing, sweeping into Beijing in 1644 from their homeland in northeast Asia.

As a foreign dynasty, they took great pains to present themselves as legitimate successors, all the while attempting to keep their customs and language distinct. For instance, they prohibited Manchu women from binding their feet, forbid Han Chinese from settling in Manchuria (unsuccessful) and forced all Chinese men to adopt the Manchu hairstyle (the queue) upon pain of death.

Despite these attempts, by the fall of the Qing dynasty, many Manchu had become indistinguishable from the northern Chinese.

殿, Shòuhuáng Diàn), built in 1749 during the reign of the Qianlong Emperor to honour his Manchu ancestors. Under the communists it served as the Children's Palace, before the halls were restored in 2018. Be sure to check out the exhibits in the rear courtyard, where you'll find a video, paintings and scale models of the rites and imperial processions. Also look for the pair of yellow-and-green glazed tile furnaces, used for burning silk and spirit tablets as offerings to deceased ancestors.

Perfect Peking Duck

EAT

Few visitors leave town without trying **Peking duck** (烤鸭, kǎoyā), the capital's most iconic dish. Its origins go back to the 14th century, when it was first listed in royal cookbooks, although nowadays most restaurants use open-fronted hung ovens, which were pioneered by **Quanjude Roast Duck** (MAP: ❺ P32 **A6**), Beijing's most famous roast-duck brand name. Quanjude also introduced the method of roasting over the wood of fruit trees to impart a perfume into the skin, and wrapping the meat in thin wheat pancakes.

When ordering a duck you can choose between a half duck (feeds two) or the whole quacker (feeds three to four); if you get the whole bird, it is often carved before you at the table. While this is taking place, whet your appetite by dipping some of the ultra-crispy skin into sugar – it's pure decadence.

When the duck is carved, it's time to assemble your pancakes. Begin by dipping two or three slices of meat into the fermented bean sauce, then place the slices at the top of the wrapper. Add some julienned cucumbers and scallions on top, and perhaps some pickled veggies and garlic sauce while you're at it. Fold the wrapper in half (a semicircle), and then fold in the sides so nothing leaks out. Voila! You're ready to enjoy the ultimate Beijing meal.

Traditionally, a light duck soup is served after you're done eating to cleanse your palate, but some restaurants serve it at the same time as the duck.

There are plenty of places to sample the delicacy: three of our favourites are Sìjì Mínfú (p51), Taste of Dadong (p51) and **Biànyífāng** (MAP: ❻ P32 **C6**). The first two have branches east of the Forbidden City; the last has a location southeast of Tiananmen Square.

Classical Music at the Egg

MUSIC VENUE

MAP: ❼ P32 **B5**

Plonked in the middle of an artificial lake like an alien spaceship, the Paul Andreu–designed **National Centre for the Performing Arts** (国家大剧院, Guójiā Dàjùyuàn; 2 Xichang'an Jie, 西长安街2号) – aka the 'Egg' – is a surreal yet spectacular venue at which to catch a performance of opera (Western and Chinese), ballet and classical music. Online booking is in Chinese only.

Even if you don't see a show, you can tour the venue during the day to admire the architecture and peek into the three concert venues.

Contemporary Creations at the National Art Museum

MUSEUM

MAP: ❽ P32 **D2**

Opened in 1963 with the personal endorsement of Mao Zedong, the

National Art Museum (中国
美术馆, Zhōngguó Měishùguǎn;
1 Wusi Dajie, 五四大街1号) was
conceived as the PRC's national
nerve centre for artistic expression.

In recent years the museum
has shaken off its reputation for
stodgy, state-supervised exhibitions
by inviting galleries from abroad
to exhibit, and at the same time
revamping its own output, often
in collaboration with Beijing's
prestigious Central Academy of
Fine Arts. There are usually
at least four exhibitions being
staged at once. It's closed Mondays.

Admire Antiques at the Guardian Art Center GALLERY

MAP: **9** P32 **E2**

China's largest auction house, the
Guardian Art Center (嘉德艺
术中心, Jiādé Yìshù Zhōngxīn; 1
Wangfujing Dajie, 王府井大街1号)
has a new home across from the
National Art Museum. The gorgeous
two-storey building is composed
of interlocking rectangular blocks,
pierced with different-sized circular
apertures and topped with glass
bricks on the upper level. Inside
you'll find an exhibition space, the
auction area, a quiet bookstore and
cafe, along with the PuXuan Hotel
and gastronomic restaurants like Fù
Chūn Jū (p53) .

It's best for its temporary
exhibits, which range from
antiques from the Forbidden City
to Qing dynasty *thangkas* from
Tibet. It usually holds auctions
twice a year.

WANGFUJING STREET

MAP: **10** P32 **E4**

One-time home to Manchu princes
and the site of Beijing's most
glamorous shopping strip back in
the Deng Xiaoping era, **Wangfujing**
(王府井大街, Wángfǔjǐng Dàjiē) is
a name that still carries weight in
China, even if there's nothing left to
see here. It is an excellent place to
grab a meal, however.

Oriental Plaza has a handy
basement food court at the exit
of Wangfujing subway – just one
stop away from Tiananmen East
on Line 1. Meanwhile, the apm
mall has a fine collection of more
upscale restaurants, like global
dumpling kings **Din Tai Fung**
(p51) and Peking duck at **Taste of
Dadong** (p51).

Master Chinese Cooking CUISINE

MAP: **11** P32 **C2**

If you've ever tried to make mapo
tofu or kung pao chicken at home,
then you know – even with a good
recipe, mastering the techniques
and balance of flavours can seem
all but impossible. Don't be
discouraged, however: you can
learn the ways of the wok and get
your dumpling-wrapping skills in
order at two long-standing cooking
schools that teach in English.

Black Sesame Kitchen
(黑芝麻厨房, Hēi Zhīmá Chúfáng;
WeChat: BlackSesameKitchen)

47

runs private classes near Jingshan Park; book ahead. Many people skip the cooking entirely, and go straight for the 10-course communal dinners (¥350). Held in a traditional courtyard with wine and beer, these meals are an excellent way to meet other travellers. Reserve.

Another school that teaches a variety of cooking styles is **The Hutong** (p66; thehutong.com). This superb cultural centre, located in the Drum Tower neighbourhood, runs five to six classes a week, revealing the secrets of hand-pulled noodles, ethnic minority cuisines as well as all the Beijing and Sichuan classics. Courses are 2½ hours long, cost ¥350 and conclude with a meal.

Get a Glimpse of Life in the Hutong   MUSEUM

Beijing's distinctive alleyways are known as *hutong*. Sheltered behind the grey-brick walls of these east–west alleyways are single-storey courtyard homes (*sìhéyuàn*), shaded by trees within. Oases from the world outside, the plain exteriors of Beijing homes were originally completely windowless to keep out the ever-present dust and bitter northern winds. Even today, this tradition of enclosed courtyards means that getting a sense of a traditional home from street level can be quite difficult.

Enter the **Shijia Hutong Museum** (MAP: **12** P32 **F3**; 史家胡同博物馆, Shǐjiā Hútóng Bówùguǎn; 24

Ancient Observatory
WILLIAM JU/SHUTTERSTOCK ©

If you've started to get the feeling that the emperor spent a lot of time running around from temple to altar to perform sacrificial rituals, well... you're right! In a nutshell, maintaining cosmic order was the emperor's job description. When natural disasters struck and society was plunged into chaos, it was generally believed that the emperor was slacking off on the job. This concept of unifying the cosmos and humankind can be seen in the Chinese character for king: 王 (wáng). As Confucius once said: 'The one who connects the three [horizontal lines] is the king' (一贯三为王). Here, the three horizontal lines (三) represent heaven, humanity and earth.

Shijia Hutong, 史家胡同24号). Here, you'll be able to see the layout of a traditional courtyard, as well as learn a bit about the disputed etymology of the word *hutong* (Mongolian or Han?) and admire scale models of the neighbourhood as it might have appeared when the the Bordered White Manchu Bannermen lived here.

Nearby is the exquisite alleyway boutique **Slow Lane** (MAP: **13** P32 **F3**; 细活裡, Xì Huó Lǐ; 13 Shijia Hutong, 史家胡同13号), which tempts with Tibetan yak-wool blankets, ceramic teaware from Jingdezhen and traditional handicrafts and jewellery.

Both are closed Mondays.

Geek Out at the Ancient Observatory
MUSEUM

MAP: **14** P32 **H5**

Astronomers have been studying the mysteries of the cosmos at this **observatory** (古观象台, Gǔ Guānxiàngtái; cnr Jianguomennei Dajie & East 2nd Ring Rd, 二环东

路建国门桥) since 1442. Crowning the 18m-high brick tower is an array of arcane astronomical instruments, mounted on carved stone plinths and embellished with bronze dragons. These include the deliciously named 'Altazimuth quadrant', which calculates the zenith distance of stars, one of six grand contraptions designed by Ferdinand Verbiest, a 17th-century Jesuit missionary from Belgium.

The observatory dates back much further to the Yuan dynasty, when it lay north of the present site. Kublai Khan, like subsequent Ming and Qing emperors, relied heavily on astronomers to plan military endeavours and fine tune the almanac. The Yuan also produced several celebrated Chinese astronomers, including Guo Shoujing, who calculated a year precisely to 365.2425 days.

At ground level are exhibits on the Chinese calendar, ancient star charts and the Jesuits.

It's closed Mondays.

🏛 THE JESUITS IN CHINA

The Jesuits were foundational figures in the exchange of knowledge and culture between Europe and China, creating some of the earliest bilingual dictionaries, atlases and cornerstone translations. Matteo Ricci (1552–1610), who came to China in 1583, eventually became an adviser to the Wanli Emperor's court and was the first European to enter the Forbidden City. During the Qing dynasty, the Manchu emperors made use of the Jesuits' knowledge of astronomy, map-making and science in order to help legitimise their reign through the spread of more accurate imperial almanacs and predictions of astronomical events like eclipses.

Meet the Ming
BUDDHIST TEMPLE

MAP: **15** P32 **H3**

Lost in a tumbledown *hutong* neighbourhood, **Zhihua Temple** (智化寺, Zhìhuà Sì; 5 Lumicang Hutong, 禄米仓胡同5号) is one of Beijing's best-preserved Ming dynasty structures. It was built in 1444 to honour a corrupt and powerful eunuch, Wang Zhen, who held tremendous sway over the guileless Emperor Zhengtong.

Remarkable treasures within include the Ten Thousand Buddhas Hall with floor-to-ceiling wall niches filled with miniature Buddhist effigies. Walk here from the Chaoyangmen subway stop.

It's closed Mondays.

Exquisite Collection of Ancient Bronzes
MUSEUM

MAP: **16** P32 **H1**

The **Poly Art Museum** (保利艺术博物馆, Bǎolì Yìshù Bówùguǎn; 14 Dongzhimen Nandajie, 东直门南大街14号保利大厦9层) is a thrilling discovery, its intimate collection of treasures hidden halfway up an office building. China's state-owned Poly Group has funnelled a fraction of its wealth into buying up Chinese antiquities from auctions overseas, displayed here on artfully lit plinths. There are ancient bronzes from the Shang and Zhou dynasties, vividly detailed Buddha statuary and four of the 12 bronze zodiac heads plundered during the 1860 sacking of the Old Summer Palace.

To get here, ride the lift to the 9th floor. It's closed Sundays.

See page 32 for map of locations

Best Places for...

✪ Budget   ✪✪ Midrange   ✪✪✪ Top End

Eating

Peking Duck

Sìjì Mínfú
四季民福 ✪✪
17 D4
Some of the best birds in town, with a prize perch overlooking the Forbidden City's moat. Dinner queues can be up to two hours. *11 Nanchizi Dajie,* 南池子大街11号

Sìjì Mínfú
四季民福 ✪✪
18 D3
Slightly less glamorous location but the same succulent duck, and still within striking distance of the Forbidden City. *32 Dengshikou Xijie,* 灯市口西街32号

Taste of Dadong (Rhapsody)
小大董 ✪✪
see **21** E4
Start with the Instagrammable appetisers at this busy

branch of maestro Dong Zhenxiang's modern restaurant. *6th fl, apm mall, 138 Wangfujing Dajie,* 王府井大街138号 apm6层

Duck de Chine 1949
全鸭季 ✪✪✪
19 F4
Beijing's most refined destination for duck. Perfectly bronzed birds are announced by chiming a gong. *98 Jinbao Jie,* 金宝街98号

Dumplings

Xiàn Lǎo Mǎn
馅老满 ✪
20 F1
A dozen varieties of delicious dumplings, including vegetarian. There are loads of other great local eats on this block, too. *316 Dongsi Beidajie,* 东四北大街316号

Din Tai Fung
鼎泰丰 ✪✪
21 E4
Line up for lovingly wrapped *xiǎolóngbāo* (Shanghai-style soup dumplings) from Taiwan's

world-famous chain. *6th fl, apm shopping mall, 138 Wangfujing Dajie,* 王府井大街138号apm6层

Budget

Yuèbīn Fànguǎn
悦宾饭馆 ✪
22 D2
This old-school canteen is a marvellous, messy microcosm of Beijing at its most boisterous. It's really hard to find – ask for directions. *43 Cuihua Hutong, off Wusi Dajie,* 五四大街翠花胡同43号

Pang Mei Noodles
胖妹面庄 ✪
23 E2
'Chubby little sister's' Chongqing noodle shop is spicy, stylish and packed tight. Shares a renovated *hutong* space with **Jing-A Longfusi** (p53) and **Susu** (p52). *Bldg A, 38 Qianliang Hutong,* 钱粮胡同38号A铺

Crescent Moon Muslim Restaurant
弯弯月亮 ✪
24 F1
Mount your culinary camel and traverse the

Peking duck
PRATAN/SHUTTERSTOCK ©

Silk Road to Uyghur-style grilled lamb, baked flatbreads and pulled noodles. *16 Dongsi Liutiao Hutong,* 东四六条胡同16号

Gourmet Lane
美食界 🅥

25 E5

Ultra-convenient food court at the Wangfujing subway stop. Noodles, hotpot and capital cuisine. One stop from Tiananmen Square. *Basement, Oriental Plaza,* 东方广场,王府井地铁站

Midrange

Chuān Bàn 川办 🅥🅥

26 H4

Originally for visiting cadres, this restaurant attached to the Sichuan provincial government office serves an encyclopaedic spice-fest of delicacies. *Gongyuan Xijie Toutiao, off Jianguomennei Dajie,* 建国门内大街贡院西街头条5号

Grandma's 外婆家 🅥🅥

27 E4

The delicious Hangzhou-style dishes at this popular chain restaurant are astonishing value. *6th fl, apm mall, 138 Wangfujing Dajie,* 王府井大街138号apm6楼

Susu 苏苏 🅥🅥

see **23** E2

Dine on Vietnamese fare such as fresh spring rolls and *phở* (beef noodle soup) at this much-loved modern *hutong* eatery. Cocktails recommended. *38 Qianliang Hutong,* 钱粮胡同38号

Gastronomic

TRB Hutong

28 D1

TRB (Temple Restaurant Beijing) serves modern European cuisine, but the real delight is the setting: the exquisite 250-year-old Temple of Wisdom. *23 Shatan Beijie, off Wusi Dajie,* 五四大街沙滩北街23号

Fù Chūn Jū

see **9** E2

Hong Kong chef Waikit Yeung sources only the finest ingredients for his lauded contemporary Cantonese dishes. *PuXuan Hotel, 1 Wangfujing Dajie,* 王府井街1号璞瑄酒店

Rive Gauche ♥♥♥

see **9** E2

Deconstructed dishes are based around a single ingredient at this clever European bistro. The slow-cooked short ribs are a sensation. *PuXuan Hotel, 1 Wangfujing Dajie,* 王府井街1号璞瑄酒店

Drinking

Bars

Jing-A Longfusi

see **23** E2

Knock back Beijing-inspired craft beers at this hip taproom, which shares a modern *hutong* development with restaurants, shops and an art gallery. *38 Qianliang Hutong,* 钱粮胡同38号

Slowboat DSK Taproom

29 F3

The good ship Slowboat has dropped anchor in central Beijing, excellent news for those in hotel-heavy Wangfujing, who now have a local brewery within stumbling range. *157 Dongsi Nandajie,* 东四南大街157号

MO Bar

30 D4

Legendary bar Hope and Sesame from Guangzhou,

voted one of Asia's best in 2019, crafted the molecular-style cocktail list at MO, an uber-glam hangout in the Mandarin Oriental. *WF Central, 269 Wangfujing Jie,* 北京王府井文华东方酒店王府井大街269号王府中环

Cafes & Teahouses

Laijin Yuxuan Teahouse
来今雨轩茶社

31 C5

The ultimate refuge from the crowds milling about the front of the Forbidden City is this historic teahouse in a corner of Zhongshan Park. Delicious steamed buns and other snacks. *Zhongshan Park,* 中山公园

Book Cafe

see **9** E2

Recharge your batteries inside this hidden cafe in the **Guardian Art Center** (p47), with plenty of illustrated art books to browse. *1 Wangfujing Dajie,* 嘉德艺术中心, 王府井大街1号

See p68
for eating
and drinking
listings

Explore
Drum Tower & Dongcheng North

Bookended by the magnificent Drum and Bell Towers in the west and Lama Temple in the east, this is Beijing's buzziest district of historic *hutong* alleyways, and the best area for strolling and cycling. Casually referred to as 'Gulou' (鼓楼; Drum Tower), come here to encounter Beijing on a refreshingly human scale as you stroll through low-rise lanes, past Beijingers playing cards or *xiangqi* (Chinese chess) and holes-in-the-wall hawking street food. Discreet cocktail bars and trendy cafes slot between grey-brick residences, while a small selection of boutique hotels make it an excellent base. After dark, you'll find a handful of alleyway spots for a drink and live music.

Getting Around

Ⓢ **Subway Line 2**
Runs east–west along the northern edge of the neighbourhood, with stops at Gulou Dajie (Drum Tower) and Lama Temple.

Ⓢ **Subway Line 5**
Runs north–south from the Lama Temple through Beixinqiao (Ghost St) and Zhangzi Zhonglu (restaurants).

Ⓢ **Subway Line 8**
Runs north–south and connects Tiananmen East with Nanguluo Xiang, Shichahai and Gulou Dajie (Drum Tower).

★
THE BEST

TEMPLE
Lama Temple (p60)

HISTORIC SIGHT
Drum Tower (p58)

FUN ON TWO WHEELS
Hutong Bike Tour (p67)

CULINARY ADVENTURE
Food Tour (p66)

LIVE MUSIC
Modernista (p69)

Bell Tower (p59)
LEONID ANDRONOV/SHUTTERSTOCK ©

	A	B	C	D

1

Jiugulou Waidajie 旧鼓楼外大街

Gulouwai Dajie

Ande Lu

Ande Lu

Andingmennwai Dajie

Hucheng River (City Moat)

North 2nd Ring Rd 二环北路

2

Gulou Dajie
鼓楼大街

Beiluogu Xiang 北锣鼓巷

Andingmen
安定门

Andingmennei Dajie 安定门内大街

Jiugulou Dajie 旧鼓楼大街

Jingtu Hutong 净土胡同

Cheniandian Hutong

3

Hong'en Temple

🏛 **3**

Zhangwang Hutong

Doufuchi Hutong 豆腐池胡同

Huafeng Hutong 华丰胡同

🎵 **26**

22
🍴 **19**

Baochao Hutong 宝钞胡同

Beiluogu Xiang 北锣鼓巷

Houyuan'ensi Hutong

14 🍴

Bell Tower
◎

4

Zhonglouwan Hutong

🍴 **9**

Drum Tower
◎

Gulou Dongdajie 鼓楼东大街

☕ **30**

🍴 **11**

24

☕ **29**

5

Shichahai
什刹海 Ⓢ

Di'anmen Waidajie 地安门外大街

Nanxiawazi Hutong 南下洼子胡同

Nanluogu Xiang 南锣鼓巷

🍴 **10**

Jiaodaokou Nandajie 交道口南大街

12 🍴

Qianhai Lake

🍺 **23**

Mao'er Hutong 帽儿胡同

Qi Baishi's Former Residence
🏛 **2**

Yu'er Hutong

🎵 **27**

Banchang Hutong 板厂胡同

Nanluogu Xiang
1

6

Di'anmen Xidajie
地安门西大街

🍴 **15**

Di'anmen Dongdajie 地安门东大街

Ⓢ 地安门东大街

Nanluogu Xiang
南锣鼓巷

Meishuguan Houjie

	A	B	C	D

E
F
G
H

500 m
0.25 miles

8 Ditan Park

Hepingli Xijie

Hucheng River (City Moat)
North 2nd Ring Rd 二环北路

Lama Temple 雍和宫
Wudaoying Hutong 五道营胡同

Lama Temple

Paoju Toutiao 炮局头条

Confucius Temple & Imperial College 4
Guozijian Jie 国子监街

Fangjia Hutong 方家胡同

Yonghegong Dajie 雍和宫大街

Hepingli Dongjie

Dongzhimen Beixiaojie

Nanguan Park

Beixinqiao Santiao Hutong 北新桥三条

Overseas Chinese History Museum 5

Beixinqiao 北新桥
Jiaodaokou Dongdajie

Dongzhimennei Dajie (Ghost St) 东直门内大街
6 Ghost Street

7 The Hutong

Dongsi Beidajie 东四北大街

Dongzhimen Nandajie

Zhangzizhong Lu 张自忠路

Zhangzizhong Lu
Dongsishitiao Lu

E
F
G
H

Drum & Bell Towers

Once the tallest buildings in Beijing, the scarlet Drum Tower and the brick-and-stone Bell Tower have kept time in the city since 1272, when they stood at the heart of the former Mongol capital of Dadu. In the Ming and Qing, they were northernmost landmarks on the central axis.

MAP P56 **A4**

PLANNING TIP

A drumming troupe stages a brief performance on replica drums every hour on the hour from 10am to 5pm; there's no performance at noon. Performances end at 4pm from November through March.

Drum Tower

Up in the 46m-high three-storey **Drum Tower** (鼓楼, Gǔlóu; Gulou Dongdajie, 鼓楼东大街), 25 massive drums were struck 108 times (18 fast beats, 18 slow beats, 18 steady beats, then repeat) to announce the closing of the city gates and the beginning of curfew at nightfall. Thereafter, every two hours (a period known as a *geng*) the drums were struck and the bell was rung to coordinate patrols of the city's nightwatch, who had their own sets of clappers and gongs. This continued until daybreak, when the city gates were again opened. When Europeans first arrived in Beijing in the 18th century, one of their chief complaints was, rather humorously, being unable to get a good night's sleep.

Accessed by a steep stairway, the tower's 2nd floor displays the Night Watchman's Drum, the sole survivor of the original 25 drums. The original drummers would have known exactly when to strike their instruments thanks to a water clock (clepsydra), a copy of which is on display in the tower. On the 1st floor is a good exhibition on traditional timekeeping in China, as well as some excellent recordings of the cries of itinerant peddlers advertising their wares over a century ago.

The current building dates to 1894.

Bell Tower
STRIPPEDPIXEL.COM/SHUTTERSTOCK ©

Bell Tower

The restrained, grey-stone edifice of the **Bell Tower** (钟楼, Zhōnglóu) stands just north of the Drum Tower; climb the steep steps to get a look at the giant 60-ton copper bell. The bell was rung after the drums were struck, also for a count of 108 times. In 1924, after Puyi (the 'Last Emperor') had been evicted from the Forbidden City, the timekeeping functions of the towers ceased.

In between the two towers is a small square, a popular destination for spry elderly Beijingers to chat in the sun, play *jianzi* (similar to juggling a football, but instead using a weighted shuttlecock) and also perform ribbon dances.

Since 1990, the bell is rung once a year on 31 December.

TAKE A BREAK
Right next to the Drum Tower is the fabulous old-school canteen Yáojì Chǎogān Diàn (姚记炒肝店), where you can sample local comfort foods like millet porridge, offal stew and steamed buns.

⭐ **TOP EXPERIENCE**

Lama Temple

The magnificent Lama Temple extends through a crescendo of evermore divine halls in a cloud of incense smoke and flowing Manchu, Tibetan and Mongolian script. Converted from a princely residence to a lamasery in the 18th century, it's a profound introduction to Tibetan Buddhist lore.

MAP P56 **F2**

PLANNING TIP

Pick up a free bundle of incense just before passing through the first gate. To say a prayer, light three sticks, bow three times, then add your lit incense to the burner. Non-Buddhists are welcome to participate.

History

The **Lama Temple** (雍和宫, Yōnghé Gōng; 12 Yonghegong Dajie, 北新桥雍和宫大街12号) started life as a royal residence, built in 1694 for the fourth son of the Kangxi Emperor. In 1744, it was converted into a lamasery for acolytes of Tibetan Buddhism. In 1792, the Qianlong Emperor, having quelled a Nepalese invasion in Tibet, instituted new rules in order to help the Manchus weaken the most powerful clans in Tibet and Mongolia.

Known as the Golden Urn system, it involved two ceremonial vessels. One was kept at Lhasa's Jokhang Temple and used to determine the reincarnations of the Dalai and Panchen Lamas, and the other was kept at the Lama Temple in Beijing and used to determine the reincarnation of the Mongolian Lama.

The First Halls

After walking the length of the Imperial Way, you'll come to the first of the temple's six main halls. This is the **Yonghe Gate**, where a plaque is inscribed with the characters 心明妙现: 'If the heart is bright, the wonderful will appear'. The next hall, the **Yonghe Hall**, contains a trinity of gilded effigies representing the past, present and future Buddhas. This is followed by the **Yongyou Hall**, which originally served as the prince's bed chamber.

Yonghe Hall
BRIAN KINNEY/SHUTTERSTOCK ©

Hall of the Wheel of the Law

A 6m-tall bronze statue of Tsongkhapa (1357–1419), founder of the Gelugpa (Yellow Hat) sect, welcomes you into the dimly lit, atmospheric **Hall of the Wheel of the Law**. A throne seated the Dalai Lamas when they lectured here; kneeling cushions attest to the hall's continued tutelary role.

Wanfu Pavilion

The grand finale is the **Wanfu Pavilion**, which reveals an awe-inspiring, 18m-tall statue of the Maitreya Buddha in its Tibetan form, clothed in yellow satin and reputedly carved from a single trunk of Tibetan sandalwood. It was a gift from the seventh Dalai Lama to the Qianlong Emperor.

It's well worth perusing the collection of Tibetan ritual objects, robes and mandalas within the side halls here, particularly Banchan Lou, formerly the chambers of the sixth Panchen Lama, who visited Beijing to celebrate the emperor's birthday in 1780.

TAKE A BREAK
Lively Wudaoying Hutong has plenty of drinking and dining options, including coffee and cake at Metal Hands. The capital's finest vegetarian fare, meanwhile, is at King's Joy.

61

WALKING TOUR

Walk the Drum Tower Hutong

A more peaceful alternative to the Nanluogu Xiang crowds, this walk meanders through the backstreets of the Drum Tower neighbourhood. During the Qing dynasty this was a particularly wealthy area, as evidenced by the many fine mansions that once largely belonged to the Manchu families of the Bordered Yellow Banner.

START	END	LENGTH
Yuhe Nunnery, Nanluogu Xiang subway stop	Drum Tower, Shichahai subway stop	2km; one hour

❶ A Renovated Temple

Begin at the graceful **Yuhe Nunnery** (玉河庵, Yùhé Ān; 49 Dongbuya Qiao Hutong, 东不压桥胡同49号), whose three compact halls were originally dedicated in 1808. It's now home to Voyage Coffee (10am to 6pm), with lovely seating both inside the compound and along the canal. It's west from the Nanluogu Xiang subway stop, along Di'anmen Dongdajie.

❷ Willow-Shaded Canal

Follow the pleasant **canal-side walkway** north. This waterway, alternately known as the Jade or Imperial River, was part of the vast waterworks project begun during the Yuan dynasty, which brought spring water from the Western Hills to the city and facilitated shipping to and from the Grand Canal to the east. This particular branch supplied water to the Forbidden City's moat.

❸ Traditional Painting Studio

Turn right at the archway marking Yu'er Hutong (雨儿胡同). Halfway down this alley is the former **home and studio of painter Qi Baishi** (1864–1957), where you can enter for a glimpse of a traditional courtyard home. There's a great gift shop.

❹ Home of the Last Empress

Retrace your steps to the canal and continue to the next *hutong*, Mao'er (帽儿胡同), where, at Nos 35 and 37, you'll find the **childhood home of Gobulo Wanrong**. A Manchu noblewoman, Wanrong married China's last emperor, Puyi, in 1922 and was unwillingly instated as empress of Manchukuo under the Japanese.

❺ Hidden Brewery

Return to Doujiao Hutong (豆角胡同) and turn right, then turn right again as it winds past the tree-shaded courtyard of **Great Leap Brewing #6**, Beijing's first craft-beer bar.

❻ Backstreet Noodles

Turn left onto Nanxiawazi Hutong (南下洼子胡同) and continue north, passing a rare sight in Beijing: a covered market, selling fresh noodles and vegetables. Across the intersection is the king of neighbourhood noodle shops: **69 Fangzhuanchang Zhajiangmian** (方砖厂69号炸酱面), which inspired a modern chain that has sprung up across the capital. Continue west down the tree-shaded **Fangzhuanchang (Brick-maker's) Hutong** until you reach Di'anmenwai Dajie (地安门外大街) and the Shichahai subway stop.

EXPERIENCES

Shopping on Nanluogu Xiang
SHOPPING

MAP: **1** P56 **C6**

Beijing's most touristy *hutong* district, **Nanluogu Xiang** (South Gong and Drum Lane) is a north–south strip of snack stalls, souvenir shops, Chinese tourists dressed as Manchu princesses and more people than you can possibly imagine on a single street – all set, rather unbelievably, to David Byrne's *The Last Emperor* theme song, which is blared on endless repeat. It can be a good time if you want to buy the odd inexpensive gift (eg The Beijing Flirtatious Expressions Map) and duck into the side streets in search of a historic residence or two. That said, if you want an idea of what a traditional *hutong* neighbourhood once looked like, follow the walking tour (p62) instead.

Traditional Art in Qi Baishi's Former Home
MUSEUM

MAP: **2** P56 **B5**

Qi Baishi (1864–1957) was a traditional Chinese painter who practised at a time when most of his peers were experimenting with European techniques. Born into an impoverished family from Hunan, Qi was often sick as a child and unable to help out with farmwork. He instead apprenticed as a carpenter, but found this equally demanding and then switched to woodcarving. It wasn't until age 25 that he began to study painting, calligraphy and seal carving.

Qi's work is instantly recognisable: his style is simple and playful, capturing the inner spirit of his subjects, usually flowers, fruit, insects and animals. Qi moved to Beijing in 1917 and rooms in this former **courtyard residence** (齐白石旧居纪念馆, Qí Báishí Jiùjū Jìniànguǎn; 13 Yu'er Hutong, 雨儿胡同13号) recreate his living quarters and studio. If you like Chinese art, the gift shop here is remarkably good. It has the highest-quality souvenirs in the Nanluogu Xiang area.

Peer into the Guan
GALLERY

MAP: **3** P56 **A3**

Before the arrival of communism, Beijing had hundreds of temples and shrines, a handful of which served as the retirement homes for palace eunuchs. **Hong'en Temple** (宏恩观, Hóng'ēn Guàn; 21 Doufuchi Hutong, 豆腐池胡同21号), just north of the Bell Tower (p59), was one such place. Initially established in the 13th century, its gradual decline over the dynasties eventually led to one palace eunuch saving it from ruin in 1873. Liu Duosheng, who was also an ordained Taoist priest, bought as many as 20 local temples during this time.

Hong'en Temple reopened in 2023 after extensive renovations and was redubbed the Guan (观).

At the time of writing it was a bit of an oddity: a small bookstore selling the collected works of Mao,

Confucianism (儒教; Rújiào) is based upon the teachings of Confucius (孔子; Kongzi), a 6th-century-BCE philosopher. The central emphasis is on five basic hierarchical relationships: father–son, ruler–subject, husband–wife, elder–younger, friend–friend. Confucius believed that if each individual carried out his or her proper role in society (ie a son served his father respectfully, while the father provided for his son), social order would be achieved.

Deng and Xi Jinping was front and centre, while China Post had opened a takeaway teashop in a side hall. Nonetheless, it's worth peeking your head in on the way to or from the Bell Tower – there's an interesting exhibit on the temple's history hidden in the back hall.

Ponder the Wisdom of the Great Sage CONFUCIAN TEMPLE

MAP: ❹ P56 **E3**

An incense stick's toss away from the Lama Temple (p60), China's second-largest **Confucius Temple** (孔庙, Kǒng Miào; 13 Guozijian Jie, 国子监街13号) is a haven of scholarly calm and contemplation. Come to wander between the towering stone stelae mounted on the backs of mythical *bìxì* (mythical, tortoise-like dragons) and inscribed with the achievements of scholars past. For centuries, China's best students would study the Confucian classics at the connecting **Guozijian** (国子监, Imperial College).

Visitors pass through the Confucius Temple first, where the emperor offered sacrifices to Confucius, before circling back through the Guozijian. In between the two is an astounding stone 'forest' of 190 stelae recording 13 Confucian classics in 630,000 Chinese characters. The Guozijian is considerably more engaging, and features illuminating displays on the imperial examinations. You won't be able to miss the Biyong Palace, a twin-roofed structure topped with a splendid gold knob, where later emperors expounded the Confucian classics to an audience of thousands of kneeling students, professors and court officials.

Built by the grandson of Kublai Khan in 1306, the former college was the supreme academy during the Yuan, Ming and Qing dynasties. Some of Beijing's last remaining *páilóu* (decorative archways) survive on the street outside (Guozijian Jie).

The temple is closed Mondays.

Overseas Chinese Communities Around the World MUSEUM

MAP: ❺ P56 **H4**

The **Overseas Chinese History Museum** (中国华侨历史博物馆, Zhōngguó Huáqiáo Lìshǐ

Bówùguǎn; Beixinqiao Santiao Dong Kou, 北新桥三条东口) charts the history of Chinese emigration from the era of the Silk Road to the present day, with full English captions throughout.

Diorama-rich exhibits look at all sides of the Chinese diaspora, from the indentured labourers sent to European colonies (particularly in the Caribbean) to gold-rush adventurers in America and Australia to the hugely influential Chinese communities in Southeast Asia.

Although it's a bit off the beaten path, this is one of the best curated museums in Beijing.

It's closed on Mondays.

Eat Your Way Through Ghost St

FOOD STREET

MAP: **6** P56 **G4**

Beijing's most raucous restaurant strip is **Ghost St** (簋街, Gui Jie; Dongzhimennei Dajie, 东直门内大街). Jammed with over 100 restaurants, it's the perfect place to join Beijingers as they let off steam.

Hú Dà (p68), with five restaurants along the 1.5km strip, is wildly popular for its Sichuan-style crayfish, with huge queues every evening. For something less spicy, Fu De Yu Hotpot (p68) is a tiny eatery specialising in Beijing-style *shuan yangrou* (mutton hotpot). Grill your own lamb skewers and other kebabs at Hěnjiǔ Yīqián Yángròu Chuàn (p68).

The original name Ghost St could derive from the ghostly lanterns illuminating a night market here during the Qing dynasty, or because corpses were transported out of the city via the Dongzhimen city gate. In the 1980s, the authorities changed the character from 鬼 to 簋, which refers to a type of ancient bronze food vessel.

Make New Friends on a Food Tour

TOUR

MAP: **7** P56 **G4**

There's no way around it: the best way to appreciate Chinese cuisine is with a group meal. For the best introduction to local food culture, join a belt-busting tour of several **hutong** eateries. Dinner tours usually take in four restaurants, all with multiple dishes and drinks, so come with an appetite. Walking is an essential part of these tours – that's good, as it gives you time to digest between courses.

A popular alternative to the dinner tour is the breakfast tour – especially if you're jet-lagged and up and ready to go in the early hours. Explore the backstreets in search of popular breakfast treats, from *jiānbǐng* (煎饼; Chinese crepes) to sour *dòuzhī* (豆汁; fermented mung-bean milk) and *jiāoquān* (焦圈; fried dough rings).

Good tour operators include **Lost Plate** (lostplate. com), **Untour Food Tours** (untourfoodtours.com) and **The Hutong** (thehutong.com).

Cycle the Alleyways
CYCLING

Beijing is one of the world's great cycling cities: it's flat as a chessboard, bike lanes are wide and ubiquitous, and shared bikes are cheap and plentiful. It's true that two-wheeled traffic can be a bit... chaotic, but as long as you have good spatial awareness and are vigilant, you'll have loads of fun.

One good way to break into **Beijing cycling** is to take a *hutong* tour, where traffic moves at a slower speed. Start at the Drum Tower and give yourself 30 to 60 minutes to explore the winding lanes as you slowly make your way 2km northeast to the Confucius Temple and Lama Temple. Trying to pick your way across the city backstreets can be a great adventure.

There are currently three companies running bike shares in Beijing. We found that the most foreigner-friendly was the blue-coloured **Hello Bike** (哈啰单车; Hāluō Dānchē); download the app and link it to Alipay. You then use Alipay to scan a bike's QR code. Before your first ride, you will need to upload your passport photo and register with a Chinese phone number – without either, you will be unable to use the bike-share scheme.

Prices are remarkably cheap: expect to pay ¥1.5 per 30 minutes, or ¥7 for a week of unlimited cycling. There is a machine-assisted translation feature within the app.

When returning the bike, make sure you are in a designated parking zone. If the bike doesn't cooperate, try manually locking it

Local Life at Ditan Park
PARK

MAP: **8** P56 **F1**

Beijing is surrounded by four heavenly altars, and the Altar of the Earth, situated in the north within **Ditan Park** (地坛公园, Dìtán Gōngyuán; Hepingli Xijie, 和平里西街), is one of them. A square open-air platform, the altar was where imperial rites were performed at summer solstice. Although not meriting a special trip, the park is a good place to see Beijingers at play, especially at the exercise area in the northeast corner.

 JIĀNBǏNG

The much-loved *jiānbǐng* is adored in Beijing, although it originates in neighbouring Tianjin. A batter of wheat flour and millet is cooked thin on a griddle, an egg (or two) cracked on top, then chilli sauce and *furu* (fermented bean curd) are lathered on with a brush, before adding coriander and onion and the all-important crunchy fried dough square. It's then folded into a sumptuous, self-contained breakfast parcel. Watching it being made is almost as fun as eating it. You can find *jiānbǐng* all over town, sold from roving bicycle kitchens or holes-in-the-wall.

See page 56 for map of locations

Best Places for...

❤ Budget ❤❤ Midrange ❤❤❤ Top End

Eating

Beijing

Yáojì Chǎogān Diàn
姚记炒肝 ❤

9 B4

Order at the counter then join the queue for Beijing's famous *chǎogān*, a glutinous stew of pig's liver and intestines. Opt for steamed buns if you don't have the guts. *311 Gulou Dongdajie,* 鼓楼东大街311号

69 Fangzhuanchang Zhajiangmian
方砖厂69号炸酱面 ❤

10 B5

Decisions are easy at this timeworn shop: the signature *zhajiang* noodles (¥25) is the only thing on the menu. Don't skip the pickled garlic. *Fangzhuanchang Hutong,* 方砖厂胡同

Yǐnsān Dòuzhī
尹三豆汁 ❤

11 D4

For a local breakfast, pop into this local chain for *dòuzhī* (fermented mung-bean milk) and fried dough rings. Branches throughout Beijing. *295 Andingmennei Dajie,* 安定门内大街295号

Budget

Zhang Mama
张妈妈川味馆 ❤

12 D5

An absurdly affordable spice-fest, humble Zhang Mama is run by a multi-generational Sichuanese family. Expect to queue. *76 Jiaodaokou Nandajie,* 交道口南大街76号

Fu De Yu Hotpot
孚德裕 ❤

13 F4

Traditional Beijing hotpot (the non-spicy variety) in coal-fired cauldrons. Cook the ingredients in the broth then dip them in sesame sauce. *264 Dongzhimennei Dajie,* 东直门内大街264号

Xiàn Lǎo Mǎn
馅老满 ❤

14 D3

The locals' pick for delicious dumplings. Veggie options, too. *252 Andingmennei Dajie,* 安定门内大街252号

Midrange

Little Yunnan
小云南 ❤❤

15 C6

Plays to the crowd with light aromatic dishes from China's southwest, like fried river fish and Dai-style mint salads. *89 Di'anmen Dongdajie,* 地安门东大街89号

Jīn Dǐng Xuān
金鼎轩 ❤❤

16 F1

Four bustling floors of great-value dim sum and Cantonese dishes by the south gate of Ditan Park. It never closes. *77 Hepingli Xijie,* 地坛南门和平里西街77号

Hú Dà 胡大饭馆 ❤❤

17 F4

Sichuan crayfish cooked in chilli-red oil, then pulled apart and gobbled up with gloved fingers. The queues are epic. *284 Dongzhimennei Dajie,* 东直门内大街284号

Hěnjiǔ Yǐqián Yángròu Chuàn
很久以前羊肉串 ❤❤

18 G4

Gather around the table-top grill for barbecued lamb skewers, chicken wings and garlic-roasted eggplant. *209 Dongzhimennei Dajie,* 东直门内大街209号

Stylish

Fúróngjì 福荣记 ⓿⓿
19 B3

Feast on modern dim sum at this upscale *hutong* restaurant. Everything on the menu is deliciously creative, from wasabi-shrimp spring rolls to curry-filled sesame puffs. *63 Baochao Hutong,* 宝钞胡同63号

King's Joy 京兆尹 ⓿⓿⓿
20 F2

Founded by chef Pan Jianjun, a former Buddhist disciple, this is the finest vegetarian meal in the city. *2 Wudaoying Hutong,* 五道营胡同2号

International

Saveurs de Corée ⓿⓿
21 H3

Bulgogi (marinated grilled beef slices), seafood pancakes, hearty *bibimbap* rice bowls and a fabulous Korean set lunch menu. *2nd fl, Rum Coabana Hotel, 22 Dongzhimen Beixiaojie,* 东直门北小街22号

Toast ⓿⓿
22 B3

Middle Eastern–inspired sharing plates draw the crowds to this stylish, all-weather rooftop restaurant. *65 Baochao Hutong,*

Gulou Dongdajie, 鼓楼东大街宝钞胡同65号

Drinking

Bars

Great Leap Brewing #6
23 B5

Lost in a maze of alleys east of Houhai, this tumbledown courtyard is where Beijing's craft-beer scene first burped into life. No food. *6 Doujiao Hutong,* 豆角胡同6号

Factory
24 C4

Chill pop-culture bar and cafe, with DJs, couches, a backroom comics shop and pizza. *135 Gulou Dongdajie,* 鼓楼东大街135号

Nuoyan Wine Bar
25 F5

Try something new at this rustic tavern specialising in Chinese wine made from glutinous rice. It's inside the People's Art Printing House compound. *7 Banqiao Nanxiang,* 板桥南巷7号

Live Music

Modernista
26 B3

Local bands, cabaret, salsa dancing and life drawing are just some of the antics unfolding

nightly at this arty Jazz Age bar. *44 Baochao Hutong,* 宝钞胡同44号

Jiāng Hú
27 D5

A hip *hutong* livehouse popular with local musicians, Jiāng Hú stages folk, blues and jazz most nights in its courtyard space. *7 Dongmianhua Hutong,* 东棉花胡同7号

Yue Space
28 F4

Check out up-and-coming Chinese bands at this arty, 500-capacity livehouse. It's inside the People's Art Printing House compound. *7 Banqiao Nanxiang,* 北新桥板桥南巷7号

Cafes

Cafe Zarah
29 D4

Ground zero for Gulou's laptop warriors, Zarah is a stylish *hutong* hangout adored for its charming staff, good coffee and potent cocktails. *46 Gulou Dongdajie,* 鼓楼东大街46号

Stillwater
30 D4

Modern design meets a traditional setting at this peaceful cafe. The rooftop terrace with *hutong* views is a great spot when it's sunny. *69 Gulou Dajie,* 鼓楼东大街69号

See p79
for eating
and drinking
listings

Explore
Temple of Heaven & Dongcheng South

A pilgrimage to the Temple of Heaven, 3km south of the Forbidden City, is as mandatory for tourists today as it was for emperors and their entourages coming here during the winter solstice to pay tribute to the gods. The temple occupies a vast tranche of real estate – prepare for lots of walking. Enticing remnants of Beijing's city fortifications are north of the temple, plus the new home of the vast imperial archives, once stored next to the Forbidden City. Immediately south of Tiananmen Square is the Qianmen Dajie shopping strip, conveying tourists along Beijing's central axis.

Getting Around

 Subway Line 2
Runs east-west along the northern edge of the neighbourhood, with stops at Qianmen (Qianmen Dajie), Chongwenmen (City Walls, Imperial Archives) and the Beijing Railway Station.

 Subway Line 5
Runs north–south. Connects lines 1 and 2 with the Temple of Heaven east gate.

 Subway Line 8
Runs north–south. Connects lines 1 and 2 with the Temple of Heaven west gate (Tianqiao stop).

Temple of Heaven (p73)
APHOTOSTORY/SHUTTERSTOCK ©

★
THE BEST

IMPERIAL ALTAR
Temple of Heaven (p73)

PEARLS
Hongqiao Pearl Market (p78)

SOUVENIRS
Qianmen Dajie (p77)

HISTORIC MAPS
First Historical
Archives of China (p78)

CITY WALLS
Southeast Corner
Watchtower (p77)

A

B Dongdan Santiao 东单三条

C

D Jianguomen 建国门

1
Tiananmen East 天安门东 Ⓢ
Dongchang'an Jie 东长安街
Wangfujing 王府井
Dongdan 东单 Ⓢ
Jianguomennei Dajie 建国门内大街 Ⓢ

Tiananmen Square

Dongdan Park

Qianmen 前门
Dongjiaomin Xiang
Chongwenmen Ⓢ
Ming City Wall Ruins Park
Ⓢ Beijingzhan Dongjie
Beijing Railway Station 北京火车站

2
Qianmen Dongdajie 前门东大街
Chongwenmen Xidajie
Chongwenmen Dongdajie 崇文门东大街
Ⓢ **7**
Ⓢ **6** Southeast Corner Watchtower 👁

First Historical Archives of China **9**
Dongxinglong Jie
Chongwenmenwai Dajie
Xihuashi Dajie
Donghuashi Dajie

Xixinglong Jie
10
See Enlargement

3
Zhushikou Dongdajie
Ciqikou Ⓢ 磁器口
Guangqumennei Dajie

Zhushikou 蒸市口
Qianmen Dajie 前门大街
Tiantan Lu 天坛路
Dongdaoshi Jie
Fahuasi Jie
North Gate
Tiyuguan Lu
Xingfu Lu

4
Tian Qiao 天桥
West Gate
Temple of Heaven Park Ⓐ
Hongqiao Pearl Market **8**
East Gate
Ⓢ Tiyuguan Lu 体育馆路
Temple of Heaven East Gate 天坛东门
Longtan Lu 龙潭路
Longtan Park

5
South Gate
Yongdingmen Dongjie 永定门东街
Nan'er Huan (South 2nd Ring Rd) 南二环
Jiegukou Lu

For more see
Top Experiences ⭐ p73
Experiences ✸ p77
Eating 🍴 p79

DASHILAR
Tóng Shēng Hé **2** 🛍
Madame Tussauds Waxworks **5** 👁
Jing Fans **3** 🛍
11
Shèng Xǐ Fú **12**
13
Dashilar Jie
Qianmen Dajie **1** 👁
Xianyukou Jie

0 —— 1 km
0 —— 0.5 miles
Ⓝ

0 —— 100 m

Temple of Heaven

A conduit to the cosmos, the Temple of Heaven (天坛, Tiāntán; Tiantan Donglu, 天坛东路) originally served as the vast stage for solemn rites performed by the emperor, who prayed here for good harvests. After 1918 it opened its gates to the public, and it remains one of the city's loveliest parks.

The Winter Solstice Ceremony

Imagine you were a commoner living in Beijing hundreds of years ago. It's the day before winter solstice, and for this reason, you are not permitted to go outside or even open your door. But maybe, being curious, you can't help but sneak a glance through the crack in your gate. This is what you might see: an enormous imperial entourage, as long as a celestial dragon, proceeding through the Outer City in total silence.

Soldiers in blue robes and round caps guard the perimeter. Past them, you can make out the red ceremonial robes of the neverending lines of officials and noblemen; their three-tiered parasols, giant fans made of peacock feathers and fluttering triangular banners in white, black, blue and yellow held high above their heads. And past them, at the centre, you catch a glimpse of the royal chariots, drawn by teams of white horses and monstrous elephants. Finally, the emperor himself passes by, carried by 10 men in a curtained 12m-long sedan chair. They are all en route to the Temple of Heaven, where the emperor will lodge in the Fasting Palace. He must abstain from all earthly pleasures before the solemn ceremony the next day, held in order to guarantee good harvests for the entire realm for the coming year.

PLANNING TIP
There are four gates to the park, one on each point of the compass; the east gate is most convenient for visitors, followed by the west gate.

Scan this QR code then scroll to the bottom of the page to book tickets for the Temple of Heaven

SYMBOLISM

Shape, sound and colour convene in symbolic harmony at the Temple of Heaven. The cosmic overtones of the place will delight numerologists, necromancers and the super-stitious – not to mention acoustic engineers and carpenters. Seen from above, the structures are round and their bases square, a pattern deriving from the ancient Chinese belief that heaven is round and earth is square.

Preparing for the Ceremony

The Temple of Heaven is not just an imperial temple, it is a massive park, dotted with 4000 wizened cypresses, which envelope the central axis of sacred halls. Entering through the east gate will take you beneath the trees and past the area where the sacrifices were prepared.

The first building you'll encounter is the **Animal Sacrifice Pavilion**, which is followed by the ornamental Long Corridor. This corridor once facilitated the transport of sacrificial animals to the **Divine Kitchen** compound, where a team of 90 cooks bustled about. Today, the kitchen buildings display ritual clothing and musical instruments. From here, the Long Corridor continues until it reaches the temple's centrepiece: the **Hall of Prayer for Good Harvests**.

Note: if you enter via the west gate, you'll pass instead the **Fasting Palace** (largely empty) and the **Divine Music Administration** (currently closed to the public).

The Hall of Prayer for Good Harvests

Rich in esoteric symbolism, this marvellous triple-eaved **circular building** is unlike any other in China. From afar you can admire the hall's unique design, capped with blue roof tiles that reflect its heavenly status. Climb the stairs to see the 28 concentric pillars and 36 inter-locking rafters that support the building – not a single nail was used in its construction. As the name suggests, this is where the emperor offered prayers for the coming year and was the last stop in the ritual. It's connected with the buildings to the south, where the sacrifices were made, via the 360m-long Danbi Bridge.

If you only have time for one stop in the Temple of Heaven, this is it. Count on at least an hour.

Imperial Vault of Heaven & Round Altar

The next building on the central axis is the **Imperial Vault of Heaven**, enclosed by a low circular wall known as the Echo Wall. Despite its splendid architecture, this was merely a storeroom, used for the divine spirit tablets and other sacrificial materials. The Echo Wall, 65m in diameter, is so named for its unique acoustic properties. A quiet word or two spoken a few feet from the wall can be heard at the opposite point on the circle.

The sacrifices themselves were made at the **Round Altar**, a raised dais open to the elements at the southern end of the axis. Arranged in three tiers, its divine geometry revolves around the imperial number nine, considered sacrosanct in imperial China.

QUICK BREAK
Just outside the park's east gate is the Hongqiao Pearl Market, which has a great food court in the basement. Options range from hotpot to spicy Hunan to Indian curries.

Imperial Vault of Heaven
V_E/SHUTTERSTOCK ©

Taichi
RICHARD ELLIS/ALAMY STOCK PHOTO ©

Taichi in the Park

The Temple of Heaven is one of Beijing's most popular parks, where early birds gather to exercise. Why not join them for a morning of taichi? Characterised by its graceful, slow-motion movements, taichi is an internal martial art that aims to relax the mind and develop inner qi (vital energy), with roots in Taoist meditation and yin-yang cosmology. English-speaking instructors are hard to find, so be sure to book your class in advance. The **San Feng Tai Chi Club** (北京三丰太极堂) teaches three styles; classes are usually held on weekends. Contact Eric at sanfengtaichi @gmail.com. Alternatively, **Bespoke Travel** offers private classes with a Shaolin-trained master (bespoketravelcompany.com).

EXPERIENCES

Strolling Qianmen Dajie

SHOPPING

MAP: **①** P72 **D6**

Running due south from the mighty Qianmen, Beijing's former front gate, was **Qianmen Dajie** (前门大街), once the main commercial thoroughfare of the Outer City.

Razed and rebuilt for the 2008 Olympics, Qianmen today consists of a short pedestrian shopping strip. More relaxed than Nanluogu Xiang (p63) and with a greater variety of shops, it's good for a short leisurely stroll, and can be combined with a walk through Dashilar (p98).

Look for traditional cloth slippers at **Tóng Shēng Hé** (同升和; No 17; MAP: **②** P72 **D5**), fans at **Jīng Fans** (京扇子, Jīngshànzi; No 35; MAP: **③** P72 **D5**) and hats at **Shèng Xī Fú** (盛锡福; No 57; MAP: **④** P72 **D6**), which has been in business since 1937.

Also on this strip is **Madame Tussauds Waxworks** (北京杜莎夫人蜡像馆, Běijīng Dùshā Fūrén Làxiàng Guǎn; No 16; MAP: **⑤** P72 **D5**), where Jackie Chan and Karl Marx welcome tourists.

If you're feeling peckish, popular snack shops include Qing dynasty dumpling purveyors **Dōuyīchù** (p79) and **Méndīng Ròubǐng** (p79), which sells takeaway meat pies.

Climb the Ruins of the City Wall

RUINS

The immense **Southeast Corner Watchtower** (东南角楼, Dōngnán Jiǎolóu; 9 Chongwenmen Dondajie, 崇文门东大街9号; MAP: **⑥** P72 **D2**) is connected to the only surviving section of Beijing's city walls.

Originally built in 1439, the tower is skewered with a formidable grid of 144 archery embrasures, able to rain fire on would-be attackers. Visitors can mount the battlements and explore the tower itself, a magnificent maze of carpentry over multiple floors, including an exhibition of historical photographs.

From the ramparts, gaze on the city wall as it flows west; in the far distance you can make out the central Qianmen Gate, which gives you some idea of just how massive the walls once were. Also keep

---

🗐 THE FOX TOWER

It was just outside the Southeast Corner Watchtower, also known as the Fox Tower, that the body of a murdered British woman, Pamela Werner, was discovered in 1937, as recounted in the true-crime novel *Midnight in Peking*. Bespoke Travel (bespoketravelcompany.com) runs the official Midnight in Peking Walking Tour, occasionally hosted by author Paul French himself.

an eye out for graffiti scratched into the tower by American and Russian soldiers during the Boxer Rebellion in 1900.

Get here by strolling the path alongside the wistful stretch of brick and stone of the **Ming City Wall Ruins Park** (明城墙遗址公园, Míng Chéngqiáng Yízhǐ Gōngyuán; MAP: **7** P72 C2), all that remains of the wall itself. This section extends for 1.2km, rising to a height of around 15m with defensive buttresses every 80m.

Browse for Freshwater Pearls

SHOPPING

MAP: **8** P72 C4

Occupying a purpose-built mall beside the Temple of Heaven's east gate, the **Hongqiao Pearl Market** (红桥市场, Hóngqiáo Shìchǎng; 9 Tiantan Lu, 天坛路9号) is a convenient place to stop for pearls, souvenirs and electronics. Though it feels comparatively polished, you'll still need your haggling hat on.

The 1st floor has the standard array of Chinese knock-offs: Louis Vuitton bags, Gucci apparel, kids' kung-fu outfits and a random assortment of T-shirts. The 2nd floor sells electronics – there are some good deals here, but you need to know what you're looking for. The namesake pearls are found on the 3rd floor. Devoted pearl shoppers can check out the quieter 4th floor as well.

By some accounts, China produces 95% of the world's cultured pearls, of which around 10% are traded at Hongqiao Pearl Market. A string of the humblest Chinese freshwater pearls will set you back about ¥300. The largest, most lustrous South Sea varieties can cost a thousand times more.

Peer into the Past at the Imperial Archives

MUSEUM

MAP: **9** P72 B2

For the past 650 years, the entirety of the court's documents were stored at the Imperial Archives on Nanchizi Dajie. In 2022, the collection was moved to the **First Historical Archives of China** (中国第一历史档案馆, Zhōngguó Dìyī Lìshǐ Dàng'àn Guǎn; 9 Qinian Dajie, 祈年大街9号; fhac.com.cn), which includes a fantastic, small exhibition space on the 3rd floor.

Expect to see treasures such as the world's largest map of dynastic China (3.86m x 4.56m; 1389), retroactively annotated in Manchurian. The Complete Map of Mountains and Rivers along the Jinsha River is another stunner: extending for 77.4m (only a tiny fraction is on display) – look closely, you can even see details like peddlers selling steamed buns to fishermen. Other documents include biographies from the Ming Military Position Selection Book, imperial edicts sent out to provincial subordinates and plenty of gorgeous reports in Manchurian, Mongolian and Chinese. Fire up your photo-translation app as there's little English. It's closed on Sundays.

Best Places for...

❷ Budget   ❷❷ Midrange   ❷❷❷ Top End

See page 72 for map of locations

Eating

Peking Duck

Bianyifang Roast Duck
便宜坊烤鸭店 ❷❷❷
10 A2

The granddaddy of duck roasting, Bianyifang uses antique closed ovens rather than hanging over a fruitwood flame. This yields juicier meat and softer skin, which eaters stuff into sesame rolls called *shaobing*. *65-77 Xianyukou Jie*, 鲜鱼口街65-77号

Quanjude Roast Duck Restaurant
前门全聚德烤鸭店 ❷❷❷
11 D5

Founded in 1864 by a poultry dealer named Yang Quanren, Quanjude is Beijing's most famous roast-duck brand. While this branch on pedestrian Qianmen Dajie is geared to tourists, it is certainly convenient. *30 Qianmen Dajie*, 前门大街30号

Dumplings & Buns

Méndīng Ròubǐng
门钉肉饼 ❷
12 D6

Allegedly one of Empress Dowager Cixi's favourite treats, the 'doornail meat pie' (so called because of its shape) is a classic Beijing takeaway snack – the pork filling is scorching hot, so eat carefully. *53 Qianmen Dajie*, 前门大街53号

Dōuyīchù
都一处 ❷❷
13 D6

The speciality at this historic spot is *shaomai*, a variety of steamed dumpling filled with lamb, shrimp or vegetables. Be prepared to queue. *38 Qianmen Dajie*, 前门大街38号

See p92
for eating
and drinking
listings

Explore Beihai Park & Xicheng North

On the shoulder of the Forbidden City, the willow-lined waters of Beihai Park and the trio of lakes that comprise Shichahai (Qianhai, Houhai and Xihai) are Beijing's answer to possessing neither river nor coastline. Excavated during massive Yuan dynasty waterworks projects, these lakes served as reservoirs for the city's drinking water and scenic gardens for the imperial family. Venture into the antique warren of *hutong* north of Fuchengmennei Dajie and you'll get a glimpse of old Beijing. Temples rise majestically above grey-tiled rooftops, holes-in-the-wall bake sesame *shaobing* bread and the soundtrack is authentically gruff Beijinghua, the local dialect.

Getting Around

⑤ Subway Line 2
Runs north–south through Xicheng, with stops at Fuchengmen (White Dagoba Temple).

⑤ Subway Line 4
Runs north–south through Xicheng, with stops at Xisi (Temple of Ancient Monarchs) and Ping'anli (Lines 6 & 19).

⑤ Subway Line 6
Runs east–west through Xicheng, with stops at Beihai Bei (Beihai Park), Ping'anli (Lines 4 & 19) and Chegongzhuang (Line 2).

⑤ Subway Line 8
Shichahai is the most convenient stop for the Qianhai and Houhai Lakes.

Beihai Park (p84)
LIU LEI/GETTY IMAGES ©

★

THE BEST

IMPERIAL PLAYGROUND
Beihai Park (p84)

BUDDHIST STUPA
Miaoying Temple (p91)

HISTORICAL ARTEFACTS
Capital Museum (p90)

REVOLUTIONARY ICON
Song Qingling (p88)

LIVE MUSIC
East Shore Jazz Bar (p90)

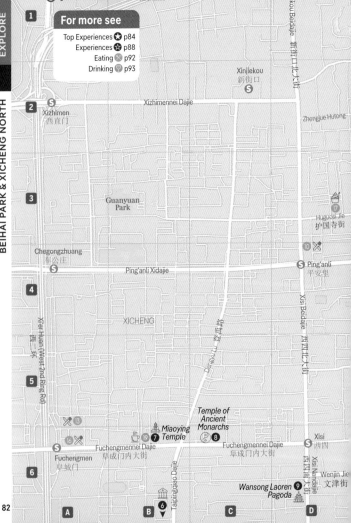

A **B** **C** **D**

1

N 0 _____ 500 m
   0 _____ 0.25 miles

For more see

Xinjiekou Beidajie 新街口北大街

Xinjiekou
新街口

2

Ⓢ
Xizhimen
西直门   Xizhimennei Dajie

Zhengjue Hutong

3

Guanyuan
Park

Huguosi Jie
护国寺街

Ⓢ

Chegongzhuang
车公庄   Ping'anli Xidajie

⑩ ✖

Ⓢ Ping'anli
平安里

4

XICHENG

Xisi Beidajie 西四北大街

5

Xi'er Huan (West 2nd Ring Rd) 西二环

Dejie山山蹄西路

✖ ⑮

⑯ ✖

Ⓢ
Fuchengmen
阜成门   Fuchengmennei Dajie
             阜成门内大街

⑲ ☕ ⚶ ⑦ Miaoying
          Temple

Temple of
Ancient
Monarchs
② ⑧

Fuchengmennei Dajie
阜成门内大街

Ⓢ Xisi
西四

Xisi Nandajie 西四南大街

6

Wenjin Jie
文津街

Wansong Laoren ⑨
Pagoda

A **B** ⑥ **C** **D**

🏛
⑥
▼

E **F** **G** **H**

Xihai Lake

1 Song Qingling's Former Residence

Deshengmenwai Dajie 德胜门外大街

Houhai Beiyan

Gulou Xidajie 鼓楼西大街

Jugulou Dajie 甘露胡同

1

Houhai Lake

Yangfang Hutong

14

Ya'er Hutong

Houhai Beiyan

Houhai Nanyan

15

2

Shichahai 什刹海

Deshengmennei Dajie 德胜门内大街

Daxianfeng Hutong

Liuyin Jie 柳荫街

Prince Gong's Mansion

2

Silver Ingot Bridge

S

12

Huguosi Jie 护国寺街

Qianhai Xijie

Fire God Temple

3

East Shore Jazz Bar ♪

4

20

Qianhai Lake

3

Di'anmenwai Dajie 地安门外大街

Slowboat Brewery

5

Beihai Bei 北海北

S

Di'anmen Xidajie 地安门西大街

Di'anmen Dongdajie 地安门东大街

Beihai Park North Gate

Gongjian Hutong 恭俭胡同

Di'anmennei Dajie 地安门内大街

4

Xishiku Dajie

Xianmen Dajie

Beihai Park

Beihai Lake

11

Di'anmen Xidajie

Xishiku Dajie 西什库大街

Beihai Park

Jingshan Houjie 景山后街

5

Jingshan Xijie

Jingshan Park

Jade Islet

Qingfeng Steamed Dumpling Shop

18

Jingshan Qianjie 景山前街

Wenjin Jie 文津街

Beihai Park South Gate

Wenjin Jie

Fuyou Jie

Wenjin Jie 文津街

Beichang Jie 北长街

6

Forbidden City

E **F** **G** **H**

Beihai Park

A royal playground for the imperial family since the Jin dynasty (1115–1234), the enclosed lake and gardens of Beihai Park (北海公园, Běihǎi Gōngyuán) still retain much of their charm. There are two main areas: the historic buildings clustered along the northwestern shore and Jade Islet in the south.

MAP P82 **G5**

PLANNING TIP

To hire a boat in summer, you'll need to pay a hefty deposit (¥400–800). Boat choices range from four-person pedal boats to six-person electric boats.

Northwestern Shore

One of several fascinating buildings along the north shore is **Jingxin Studio** (静心斋, Jìngxīn Zhāi), a 'garden within a garden' and a favourite retreat of the Qianlong Emperor, who would sip tea, listen to the plucking of the *guqin* (Chinese zither) and savour the carp-filled pools and scenic views.

Western Heaven (西天梵境, Xītiān Fánjìng) was a lamasery during the Ming dynasty, and was subsequently rebuilt in 1759; it's fronted by a magnificent four-pillared memorial arch. Beyond the Hall of the Heavenly Kings is its centrepiece, a gorgeous Ming-era hall of unpainted cedar. Nearby is the **Nine Dragon Screen**, a 27m-long spirit wall emblazoned with coiled dragons.

At the northwest corner of the lake, the Ming dynasty **Five Dragon Pavilions** (五龙亭, Wǔlóng Tíng), which jut out over the water, were a fishing spot for emperors; nowadays they're the haunt of ballroom-dancing couples. Close by, **Little Western Heaven** (小西天, Xiǎoxītiān) is the largest square pavilion-style palace in China. It was built in secret as a gift for the Qianlong Emperor's mother on her 80th birthday. Ferries (¥20) run between the North Shore and Jade Islet, or you can walk.

Bridge to Jade Islet
GUSTAVO MONIZ FERREIRA/SHUTTERSTOCK ©

Jade Islet

Shaped from the earth scooped out to create Beihai
Lake, the steep **Jade Islet** (琼华岛, Qiónghuá Dǎo)
is crowned with the 36m-high Tibetan-style White
Dagoba, built in 1651 by the first Qing emperor to
honour a visit by the Dalai Lama. While you can
access the islet from the west, it's best to enter via
the south gate. This approach allows you to enter
via **Yong'an Temple** (永安寺, Yǒngān Sì), which
extends up the steep southern slope to the summit.

The circular fortress known as **Round City**
(团城, Tuán Chéng) just outside the south gate of
Beihai was the site of Kublai Khan's palace in the
Yuan dynasty. All that survives are a few wizened
old cypress trees and a humongous, ceremonial
wine vessel made of green jade dating from 1265.
It's on display in front of the Hall of Divine Light,
which has a 1.5m-tall statue of Sakyamuni, made
from Burmese white jade. In winter, ice skating
takes place south of Jade Islet.

QUICK BREAK
Qingfeng Steamed
Dumpling Shop
(庆丰包子铺,
Qìngfēng Bāozǐ Pù)
on the southern
side of Jade Islet
is the only place to
eat inside the park.

85

WALKING TOUR

A Stroll Around Houhai

Houhai (the Back Sea; 后海) is the willow-lined lake north of Qianhai (the Front Sea; 前海) and Beihai Park. Under the Mongols (1279–1368) it marked the northern terminus of the Grand Canal; later it became a royal retreat during the Qing dynasty as Manchu nobles built mansions along its shores. Crowds converge at the Silver Ingot Bridge.

START	END	LENGTH
Silver Ingot Bridge	Silver Ingot Bridge	3km; 1½ hours

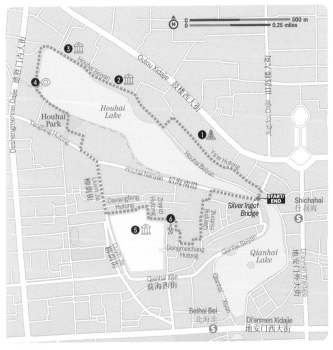

1 A Neighbourhood Temple

Going north from the bridge, turn left into peaceful Ya'er Hutong, where after a few hundred metres you'll reach **Guanghua Temple**, a working Buddhist temple dating from the far-off Yuan dynasty (closed to visitors). As the *hutong* bears sharp right, turn left (at No 46) along a narrow alley, which will take you to the lakeside.

2 The Last Emperor

Turn right at the lake and push on past **Prince Zaifeng's former stables** (at No 43) and **Prince Chun's Mansion** (at No 44), where China's last emperor, Puyi, was born.

3 The Mother of Modern China

Next up is **Song Qingling's Former Residence**, where Madame Song, the wife of Sun Yatsen, lived during the 1960s and 1970s. A revolutionary herself, she permanently broke with her family and sided with the communists during the civil war. Song Qingling held several senior positions in the government in the 1970s, even though she was never a member of the Communist Party.

4 Boats & Ballroom Dancing

Follow the lake anticlockwise, passing the training site of the **Beijing International Dragon Boat team**, until you reach a small public square called Houhai Park, a popular spot for plaza dancing in the evenings. Take the access ramp at the far-right-hand corner of the square then leave the park by heading straight on (south) to Yangfang Hutong.

5 Princely Mansion

Turn left into the *hutong,* then right into Liuyin Jie and left into Daxiangfeng Hutong, following the looming grey-brick back wall of **Prince Gong's Mansion**. Prince Gong was the Prince Regent under the Empress Dowager Cixi, and ran the Qing dynasty's foreign ministry. His was the finest lakeside residence in Beijing in the 19th century.

6 Hutong Hopping

Now the *hutong* fun begins: turn right (still following the big wall) into **Zhanzi Hutong**, bear left, but then go straight on as the *hutong* bears right, and turn right at the very end into the narrowest of alleys. Wind your way down this alley, before taking the first left onto **Dongmeichang Hutong**. Bear left, then right, then turn left at the *hutong* crossroads onto **Qianjing Hutong**, following it back to the lake.

EXPERIENCES

The Home of Song Qingling

MUSEUM

MAP: **1** P82 **F1**

As Mao Zedong once quipped, the influential Charlie Soong had three daughters: one loved money (Ailing), one loved power (Meiling), but only Qingling loved her country. Song Qingling (1893–1981) grew up in Shanghai, went to university in the US, married exiled revolutionary Sun Yatsen in Japan, and played an instrumental role in the communist government. She often represented China abroad and, after Mao's death, held several senior leadership positions. Her **residence** (宋庆龄故居, Sòng Qìnglíng Gùjū; 46 Houhai Beiyan, 后海北沿46号) is set in the gardens of the former mansion of Prince Chun. The highlight is a two-storey side hall that presents a chronological exhibit of her life, as seen through photos, letters and personal items, including her 1950s ZIS sedan – a gift from Joseph Stalin. Also worth checking out is the main residence; four of the rooms are open to the public.

Prince Gong's Mansion
SANGA PARK/SHUTTERSTOCK ©

Dream of the Red Chamber
HISTORIC BUILDING

MAP: **2** P82 **F3**

Reputed to be the model for Chinese writer Cao Xueqin's 18th-century literary masterpiece *Dream of the Red Chamber*, this sprawling residence is one of Beijing's largest traditional **mansions** (恭王府, Gōng Wángfǔ; 17 Qianhai Xijie, 前海西街17号). Little wonder that it was once owned by Prince Gong (1833–98), half-brother of the Xianfeng Emperor. While there are plenty of courtyards to explore, it's most notable for its marvellous back gardens, which feature artificial hills, ponds, rockeries, whimsical pavilions and even a Great Wall folly. Be warned that it is often wall-to-wall with tour groups, which can detract from the overall experience. Go early.

Find Your Match at the Fire God Temple
TAOIST TEMPLE

MAP: **3** P82 **H3**

On the weekend, the otherwise unremarkable **Fire God Temple** (火德真君庙, Huǒdé Zhēnjūn Miào; 77 Di'anmenwai Dajie, 地安门外大街77号) is one of the most popular temples in the capital. The main attraction is the adjacent side halls dedicated to a Fox Fairy (狐仙殿) and the Old Man under the Moon (月老殿), both of whom bestow blessings in the Marriage Department in the heavenly realms. On a busy day, you'll likely see long queues of young Chinese waiting to enter for their turn to pray and, hopefully, get a divine introduction to their perfect match.

The God of Wealth hall in the back is another popular stop for worshippers, while the main hall dedicated to the Fire God occasionally hosts Taoist musicians, who perform ritual music to accompany the various blessings.

There's been a Fire God Temple on this site since 632, but the current incarnation dates to 2007.

ZHONGNANHAI
The lakeside compound south of Beihai is known as Zhongnanhai, the modern-day Forbidden City where the senior cadres of the Chinese Communist Party (CCP) work and, in theory, reside. Understandably, if you unwittingly approach this area you will be quickly shooed away. Cashing in on Zhongnanhai's prestige is the cigarette brand of the same name, whose smokes were originally produced exclusively for Mao and other senior cadres. It's since become a popular choice among younger Chinese.

Nightlife at the Lake
DRINKING

After dark, the Houhai Lakes scenic area around Silver Ingot Bridge morphs into a neon-lit

ICE CAPADES
Winter fun at Houhai is wildly popular and not limited to ice skating. You can also hire ice trikes, their front wheels replaced with skis, and push-along ice sleds. Afterwards, it's customary to eat *tánghúlú* (糖葫芦), candied hawthorn fruit on sticks.

nightlife zone. Most bars have live music, dice games, big-screen mobile-phone gaming and KTV. In a bid to outcompete neighbouring venues, sound systems are often cranked up to 11: depending on your tastes, this is either great fun or a full-on sensory assault on your nervous system.

For a more sophisticated tipple, head to **East Shore Jazz Bar** (MAP: 4 P82 **H3**; 东岸爵士吧, Dōngàn Juéshì Bā; 2nd fl, 2 Qianhai Nanyan, 什刹海南沿2号楼2层; 3pm to 1am Tuesday to Sunday). Rock star Cui Jian's saxophonist opened this dark and moody upstairs den. It's a great place to unwind to upright bass and saxophone solos and also has fantastic views out over the water. A small roof terrace opens in summer. Musicians perform Thursday to Sunday from 9pm.

For a simple beer without the open mic, try the two-floor **Slowboat Brewery** (MAP: 5 P82 **G3**; 悠航鲜啤, Yōuháng Xiānpí; Bldg 2, Hehua Market, Shangye Jie, 荷花市场内商业街2幢), which has 45 brews on tap and more great views of Qianhai Lake.

Uncover Beijing's History MUSEUM
MAP: 6 P82 **B6**

Behind the captivating facade of the **Capital Museum** (首都博物馆, Shǒudū Bówùguǎn; Fuxingmenwai Dajie, 复兴门外大街16号) are intriguing galleries with a good overview of Beijing's history. Scale models, maps, multimedia displays and artefacts keep visitors engaged, and the English captions are helpful, though not always present. The best displays are on the 2nd and 3rd floors.

The 2nd floor stretches from the Paleolithic (Peking Man) to the Liao (916–1125) and Jin (1115–1234) dynasties, when Beijing was under the control of the Khitan (nomads from the northern steppe) and the Jurchen (ancestors of the Manchus) respectively. The Jurchen were the first to make Beijing a capital city.

The 3rd floor covers the Yuan, Ming and Qing dynasties, followed by the Republican era and the Japanese invasion. Other floors explore Beijing opera and folk customs as seen through seasonal festivals. Exhibits have a decent amount of information without being overwhelming. Plan on spending about two hours here.

To get here, take line 1 to Muxidi. It's closed on Mondays.

Pilgrimage to a Tibetan Stupa

BUDDHIST TEMPLE

MAP: **7** P82 **B6**

Originally built in 1271 under the reign of Kublai Khan, the serene **Miaoying Temple** (妙应寺白塔, Miàoyīng Sì Báitǎ; 171 Fuchengmennei Dajie, 阜成门内大街171号) slumbers beneath its astonishingly high white dagoba, the tallest in China. A glimpse of it rising imperiously above surrounding *hutong* is one of the most emotive sights in Beijing. The dagoba was built on the site of an earlier temple by a Nepali architect, invited to Dadu (as Beijing was then known) by the Khan to cement the new dynasty's relations with Tibet. You can't enter it, but you can circle the base and explore the temple halls, the largest of which, the Hall of the Great Enlightened One, has a display of Buddhist statuary. The Hall of the Seven Buddhas houses scale models presenting the Yuan dynasty cities of Dadu (Beijing), Shangdu ('Xanadu' of Coleridge's famous poem) and Zhongdu, another Yuan-era city between the other two. The *hutong* to the north and east of the temple are well worth a stroll after your visit.

Xicheng Temple Tour

TEMPLES

Beijing's quirkiest historic temples are in Xicheng, west of Beihai Park. If you're already headed to Miaoying Temple (p91), it might be worth tracking down these two other gems.

The unusual **Temple of Ancient Monarchs** (MAP: **8** P82 **C6**; 历代帝王庙, Lìdài Dìwáng Miào; 131 Fuchengmennei Dajie, 阜成门内大街131号) was constructed in 1530, and is where emperors would come to honour their royal predecessors, dating all the way back into the mists of antiquity. There were originally 188 spirit tablets on display in the massive Jingde Chongsheng Palace.

For a more intimate experience, visit the forgotten **Wansong Laoren Pagoda** (MAP: **9** P82 **D6**; 万松老人塔, Wàn Sōng Lǎorén Tǎ; 43 Xisi Nandajie, 西四南大街43号). Dating to the Mongol Yuan dynasty, this nine-tiered brick pagoda sits in a lovely walled garden of pomegranate trees and grapevines, with a hotch-potch of historical *hutong* timber frames and stone carvings scattered about. A bookshop sells old postcards and pots of jasmine tea.

See page 82 for map of locations

Best Places for...

🅑 Budget 🅑🅑 Midrange 🅑🅑🅑 Top End

Eating

Northern Chinese

Liǔ Quán Jū
柳泉居 🅑🅑

10 D4

An old-timer that's been around since 1567, when it used to be a winehouse. Bustling local atmosphere and Shandong fare. *172-178 Xinjiekou Dajie*, 新街口南大街172-178号

Royal Icehouse
皇家冰窖小院 🅑🅑

11 H4

This intriguing restaurant was once a royal refrigerator, its arched stone cellars built to store oversized ice cubes cut from Beihai Lake. *5 Gongjian Wuxiang, Gongjian Hutong*, 恭俭胡同5巷5号

Mǔmén Jiā Shuànròu
姆们家涮肉 🅑🅑

12 H3

This old Beijing-style lamb hotpot hits the spot. Next to Shichahai subway station (Exit A1). *2nd fl, 31 Di'anmenwai Dajie*, 地安门外大街31号二层

Gastronomic

Yúfúnán 渔芙南 🅑🅑

13 A5

This insanely stylish Hunan spice fest is one of the capital's best modern Chinese dining experiences. *49 Gongmenkou Toutiao*, 宫门口头条49号

Fork by TRB
福客牛排 🅑🅑🅑

14 F2

Upscale fusion tucked away in a hotel compound on Houhai's southern shores. *Blossom House, 9 Yangfang Hutong*, 羊房胡同9号花间堂后海酒店

Street Food

Yā'er Lǐjì 鸦儿李记 🅑

15 H2

For proper Hui Muslim eats, sniff out this venerable establishment in a *hutong* north of Houhai Lake. Two other Lǐjì are nearby; this is the one you want. *Ya'er Hutong*, 鸦儿胡同 (烟袋斜街西口)

Royal Palace Crisp Beef Pies
宫廷香酥牛肉饼 🅑

16 A6

This hole-in-the-wall bakes 'royal crispy beef pies', a Tang dynasty treat filled with beef, leeks and Sichuan peppercorns. *341 Fuchengmennei Dajie*, 阜成门内大街341号

Huguosi Snacks
护国寺小吃 🅑

17 D3

A time capsule of a canteen dishing up traditional sweet and savoury snacks. *93 Huguosi Jie*, 护国寺街93号

Liǔ Quán Jū

Drinking
Tea & Cafes

1901 Cafe
18 E6

A baroque three-storey cafe that's a late-Qing gem. *101 Xi'anmen Dajie,* 西安门大街101

Pagoda Light Cafe
19 B6

Popular rooftop cafe with a side order of eye candy: the towering white dagoba next door. *Pagoda Light Hotel, 185 Fuchengmennei Dajie,* 阜成门内大街185号,白塔之光酒店

Tangren Teahouse
20 H3

Commanding fine views across Qianhai Lake from its rooftop terrace, this teahouse is away from the noisier bars. Prices are high but the location, service and ambience compensate for this. 前海南沿15号

See p104
for eating,
drinking and
shopping
listings

Explore Dashilar & Xicheng South

Like many ancient Chinese capitals, Beijing was originally divided into an Inner City and Outer City, and it was at Qianmen (the Front Gate) that those two worlds met. Just beyond Qianmen was the bustling commercial district of Dashilar (大栅栏儿) filled with artisans, peddlers and an endless array of travellers. Dashilar was also an entertainment district known for theatres and more illicit pleasures, a tradition that continued well into the Republican era. Today, the shopping streets of Dashilar and nearby Liulichang are the best areas for browsing traditional Chinese goods like silk and tea, and catching a Peking opera performance.

Getting Around

 Subway Line 2
Runs east-west, with a stop at Qianmen, the most convenient hub for the neighbourhood.

Subway Line 7
Runs east-west with stops at Hufangqiao (Huguang Guild Hall), Guang'anmennei (Niu Jie Mosque) and Wanzi (Maliandao Tea Market).

 Subway Line 8
Runs north-south beneath Qianmen Dajie, with stops at Tianqiao (Ancient Architecture Museum, Tianqiao Performing Arts Centre).

Qianmen Dajie
CHUYUSS/SHUTTERSTOCK ©

THE BEST

HUTONG TOUR
Beijing Postcards (p100)

SHOPPING
Walk Dashilar (p98)

OOLONG TEA
Maliandao Tea Market (p101)

BUDDHIST PAGODA
Tianning Temple (p101)

PEKING OPERA
Huguang Guild Hall (p102)

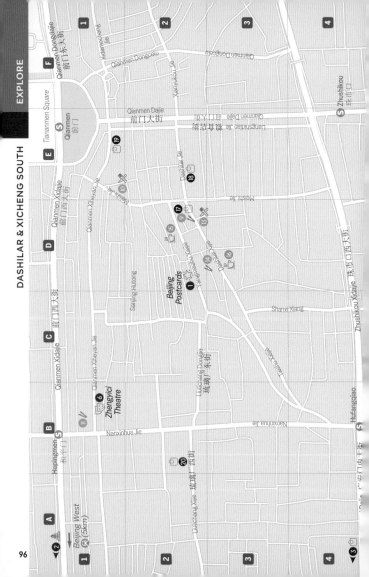

EXPLORE

DASHILAR & XICHENG SOUTH

1 Tiananmen Square

F 前门东大街 Qianmen Dongdajie

1 Xidamochang Jie

Qianmen Dongcelu

Qianmen Dongdajie

2

Qianmen Dongcelu

Xianyukou Jie

3 Zhushikou 珠市口

4

S Qianmen 前门

Qianmen Dajie 前门大街

Langfangtou Jie 廊房头条

Qianmen Dajie 前门大街

19 **E**

Dashilar Jie

18 Meishi Jie

17
6 **15** Yangmeizhu Xiejie
13

E

前门西大街 Qianmen Xidajie

Qianmen Xihecan Jie

Meishi Jie

D

14
Dashilan Jie
16

Zhushikou Xidajie 珠市口西大街

S Hepingmen 和平门

前门西大街 Qianmen Xidajie

Sanjing Hutong

Beijing Postcards

1

Shanxi Xiang

Zhushikou Xidajie 珠市口西大街

C

Qianmen Xidajie 前门西大街

Qianmen Xiheyan Jie

Lvshi Xijie

Hufangqiao

S

B Qianmen Xidajie 前门西大街

11
6
Zhengyici Theatre

Liulichang Dongjie 琉璃厂东街

Nanxinhua Jie

S

Nanxinhua Jie

A Beijing West 🚉 (5km)

Qianmen Xiheyan Jie

20

Liulichang Xijie 琉璃厂西街

1

2

3

4

Tianamen Square

Qianmen Xidajie

5

6

7

8

F

E

D

C

B

A

Temple of Heaven Park

Qianmen Dajie 前门大街

Tianqiao Nandajie 天桥南大街

S Tianqiao 天桥

Tianqiao 7 Performing Arts Centre

Xinnong Jie

Xiannongtan Jie

Yong'an Lu

Beiwei Lu 北纬路

Nanwei Lu

Dongjing Lu

Dongjing Lu

Ancient Architecture Museum 4

Xijing Lu

Xijing Lu

Yong'an Lu

Beiwei Lu 北纬路

500 m

0.25 miles

Hufang Lu

Hufang Lu

Huguang 5 Guild Hall

Fengfangliuti Jie

Fengfangliuti Jie

Nanheng Dongjie 南横东街

For more see

Experiences ✪ p100
Eating ✷ p104
Drinking ☕ p104
Shopping 🛍 p105

5

6

7

8

N

🏃 **WALKING TOUR**

Walk Dashilar

During the Qing dynasty, only the Manchu were permitted to live inside the Inner City walls. Dashilar was just beyond the main gate and part of the Outer (Chinese) City, a bustling area of commerce and entertainment. Despite being thoroughly scrubbed by the communists, the area's crooked alleys have recovered their mojo.

START	END	LENGTH
Qianmen Dajie Arch	Liulichang Xijie	2.5km; 1½ hours

❶ The Front Gate

In imperial times, the entrances to different neighbourhoods in Chinese cities were marked with a wooden *páilóu* (牌楼), or decorative archway, a vestige of the Tang dynasty when each city ward had a gate that was closed at night (in fact, Beijing's *hutong* continued to be gated off at night through the Qing dynasty).

Few *páilóu* have survived into the present day, but in some places they have been rebuilt, as is the case at the pedestrian **Qianmen Dajie** shopping street (p77).

❷ Silk Shop

Walk a few blocks down Qianmen, then turn right onto the busy cross street of Dashilar (also pronounced 'Dazhalan'). On your right at No 5 is **Ruifuxiang Silk**, East China's esteemed silk-clothing merchants, who have been trading here since 1893, and stitched the flag that was raised aloft at Tiananmen in 1949 when Mao proclaimed the founding of the PRC.

❸ Historic Cinema

At No 24 is Tongrentang, a former royal dispensary that still peddles traditional Chinese prescriptions. The first film in China was screened at No 36, **Daguanlou Cinema**, back in 1905. You can still catch a flick in the same spot, although the cinema was largely rebuilt in 2005.

❹ Pottery Shards and Jewellery

Cross Meishi Jie, turn right and enter the first alleyway on your left, Yangmeizhu Xiejie, a former printing street once home to author Lu Xun. The **Caicifang Porcelain Workshop** at No 35 upcycles shards of porcelain vases smashed during the Cultural Revolution into unique souvenirs.

❺ Postcards from the Past

Further along at No 97, pop in for a chat with the history buffs at **Beijing Postcards** (p100), who have a wealth of info on the area, displays of old Beijing maps and photographs and some cool souvenirs.

❻ Art & Antiques

Where the alleyway forks, bear right, right again and then first left (west) on to **Liulichang Culture Street**. A long strip of art stores, antiques and booksellers, Liulichang began attracting scholars during the Ming dynasty, and became a favourite destination for out-of-town students who came to the capital to take the imperial exams.

EXPERIENCES

Walking Tours with Beijing Postcards

TOUR

MAP: **1** P96 **D2**

The capital's best purveyor of history tours in English, **Beijing Postcards** (bjpostcards.com; 97 Yangmeizhu Xijie, 杨梅竹斜街97号) hosts a range of rigorously researched walks led by Danish co-founder Lars. The best of the bunch are the History of the Hutong and the Crash Course to the Forbidden City, both of which open a doorway to a world that would be impossible to find. Make sure you book far in advance.

Several walks start and end at Beijing Postcards' HQ in a Dashilar *hutong,* which doubles as a gallery and gift shop. As well as browsing photographs and images related to the latest historical research, you can purchase reprints of old city maps, and photographs and illustrations depicting a Beijing filled with imperial processions, camels and towering ramparts. Other great gifts include cushions, tote bags and calendars, all emblazoned with postcard images of old Beijing, collected by Lars and his co-founder, from markets and auctions both in China and overseas.

Additional events, including the Historical Movie Night and Historical Book Club, are worth checking out.

National Peking Opera Compnay

TESTING/SHUTTERSTOCK ©

Despite its mystique, Peking opera (*jīngjù*, 京剧) is relatively easy to follow. Common themes include intrigues, disasters and rebellions, and many narratives have their source in the stock characters and legends of classical literature. Performers substitute elaborate sets for highly symbolic moves, gesture and facial expressions. A flick of a silk tassel indicates an actor riding a horse, while lifting a foot means going through a doorway. The undisputed king of Peking opera was Mei Lanfang. Mei, who died in 1961, made his name playing female roles and introduced the world to China's most famous art form via overseas tours.

Pray for Peace at Beijing's Oldest Building
BUDDHIST PAGODA

MAP: **2** P96 **A1**

Dating back to the days when the Khitan ruled Beijing, the pagoda in the little-visited **Tianning Temple** (天宁寺, Tiānníng Sì; 3 Tianningsi Qianjie, 天宁寺前街中3号) is not only the oldest religious structure in Beijing (c 1120), it's the most impressive. The octagonal tower stands at a neck-craning 57.8m tall, and has 13 eaves and gorgeous bas-relief carvings running around the exterior. Southwest of the city centre, the temple is a bit of a hike from most places. The closest subway stop is Daguanying (lines 7 and 16); it's easiest to take a taxi.

Tea Tasting at the Maliandao Market
TEA

MAP: **3** P96 **A4**

The **Maliandao Tea Market** (马连道茶城, Mǎliándào Cháchéng; 11 Maliandao Lu, 马连道路11号) is a nondescript commercial centre home to, if not all the tea in China, then an awful lot of it. For those looking to venture beyond Beijing's favourite jasmine tea, it can be a fascinating, caffeine-fuelled excursion. To get the most out of a trip, taste several teas. Just remember that you are expected to make a purchase afterwards. Tea is sold by the gram (*kè*, 克). The smallest amount you can buy is 50 grams; an average purchase is 100 grams. The different types of tea on sale include green (*lǜchá*, 绿茶), oolong (*wūlóng*, 乌龙), black (*hóngchá*, 红茶), pǔ'ěr (普洱) and jasmine (*mòlìhuā*, 茉莉花).

A typical tasting involves sitting with your host (usually from Fujian province, where a lot of China's tea is grown) while they steep the tea multiple times and you enjoy thimble-sized cups together. To get the most out of the experience, bring along a Chinese speaker or sign up for a tea tour with the Hutong (p66). You'll also find tea sets and accessories sold at cheaper prices than elsewhere. To get here, take subway line 7 to Wanzi.

Long before the Mongols and Manchus set up camp in Beijing, there were the Khitan, a nomadic people who conquered the part of northern China then known as the 16 Prefectures. Declaring their own Liao dynasty (907–1125), the Khitan incorporated elements of Chinese bureaucracy into their state, and developed not one but two writing systems (based on Chinese and Uyghur). Eventually, China's Song government mistakenly allied with the Jurchen of Manchuria in an effort to reclaim their territory. The Jurchen responded by going on to defeat both the Khitan and the Chinese in one fell swoop. Their dynasty, the Jin (1115–1234), was the first to make Beijing a capital city.

Carpentry & Construction in the Middle Kingdom   MUSEUM

MAP: ❹ P96 D8

More than just another imperial sacrificial site, the **Ancient Architecture Museum** (北京古代建筑博物馆; Běijīng Gǔdài Jiànzhù Bówùguǎn; 21 Dongjing Lu, 东经路21号) is a compelling exploration of traditional Chinese building techniques. Examine a scale model of a temple construction site, compare the similarities of Chinese wood-working tools with those languishing in your own garage and dive into the regional differences in *dougong* (brackets), *sunmao* (joints) and courtyard homes from around the realm.

The museum is set in the former Temple of Agriculture, where the emperor was required to appear once a year during the Ming dynasty in order to plough a sacrificial field (he only had to plough three furrows, after which various ministers took over the task).

It's closed on Mondays.

Farewell My Concubine   CHINESE OPERA

Historically home to dozens of theatres, the former pleasure district of Dashilar is still a good place to see a traditional opera.

One of the most authentic venues in town is the **Huguang Guild Hall** (MAP: ❺ P96 B5; 湖广会馆, Húguǎng Huìguǎn; 3 Hufang Lu, 虎坊路3号), one of Beijing's few surviving *huiguan* (guild halls), which were ostensibly a home away from home for visiting provincial merchants and officials – in this case from Hubei and Hunan. Founded in 1807, it was converted to a theatre a few decades later. Operas play out on an elaborate canopied stage enclosed by balconies.

At the time of research, there was only one performance per week, on Saturdays at 2pm. Another traditional venue is the two-storey **Zhengyici Theatre** (MAP: ❻ P96 B1; 正乙祠戏楼, Zhèngyǐcí Xìlóu; 220 Qianmen Xiheyan, 前门西河沿220号),

Zhengyici Theatre
DEREK BROWN /ALAMY STOCK PHOTO ©

originally dating to 1668. Only one performance was being staged a week, on Fridays at 7.30pm. For a more contemporary experience, try the **Tianqiao Performing Arts Centre** (MAP: ❼ P96 **E7**; 天桥艺术中心, Tiānqiáo Yìshù Zhōngxīn; 9 Tianqiao Nandajie, 天桥南大街9号), which has 1600 seats and a variety of daily performances.

Finally, note that while the **Lao She Teahouse** (老舍茶馆, Lǎoshè Cháguǎn; 3 Qianmen Xidajie, 前门西大街3号) sounds promising, the performances here are of low quality and not recommended.

Contact for all theatres is via WeChat; there is no English.

Beijing's Muslim Community   MOSQUE

MAP: ❽ P96 **A6**

Dating from the 10th century, Beijing's oldest mosque, **Niu Jie** (牛街礼拜寺, Niú Jiē Lǐbài Sì; 18 Niu Jie, 牛街18号) is more like a Chinese temple with Islamic characteristics. Domes and minarets are conspi-cuously absent, but it does have a fine prayer hall serving the local community of Hui Chinese Muslims, who also run the many halal restaurants along Ox St (Niu Jie), such as Jùbǎoyuán (p104).

Although the Hui are listed as an ethnic group (Beijing's largest), they are culturally close to the Han Chinese, unlike the Uyghurs, who speak a Turkic language. Hui origins in China can be traced back to Persian missionaries, and later to Islamic soldiers from Central Asia fighting for the Mongol Yuan dynasty that conquered China in 1279. The mosque is lively with worshippers on Fridays, although non-Muslims are forbidden to enter during prayer.

Dress appropriately (no shorts or short skirts). Take subway line 7 to Guang'anmennei.

Best Places for...

See page 96 for map of locations

❶ Budget   ❶❶ Midrange   ❶❶❶ Top End

Eating

Gourmet

Suzuki Kitchen
铃木食堂 ❶❶
9 D2

Japanese comfort food in a beguiling *hutong* setting. *10-14 Yangmeizhu Xiejie,* 杨梅竹斜街 *10-14号*

Ms Na 私房菜 ❶❶❶
10 E1

Innovative cuisine like rose-scented duck, and a lovely outdoor terrace. *4th fl, bldg 6, Beijing Fun, 21 Langfang Toutiao,* 廊房头条21号北京坊6楼

Quanjude Roast Duck
全聚德和平门店 ❶❶❶
11 B1

This seven-floor emporium, its 41 dining rooms bedecked in communist-chic decor, is the flagship of China's most famous roast-duck brand. *14 Qianmen Xidajie,* 前门西大街14楼

Local Eats

Jùbǎoyuán 聚宝源 ❶
12 A6

A culinary destination across from Beijing's oldest mosque – queue for traditional lamb hotpot. *5-2 Niu Jie,* 牛街 *5-2号*

Wèi Dàdà Biángbiáng Miàn
魏大大biangbiang面 ❶❶
13 D2

Spicy wide-belt Shaanxi noodle specialists; look for 58-stroke *biáng,* one of the most complicated Chinese characters. *32 Dashilar Xijie,* 大栅栏西街32号

Deyuan Roast Duck
德缘烤鸭店 ❶❶
14 D3

Beijing's trinity of trad meats: Peking duck, roast lamb and donkey. Crack open a cold Yanjing beer and loosen your belt. Great value. *57 Dashilar Xijie,* 大栅栏西街57号

Drinking

Cafes

Soloist Coffee Co
15 D2

Once a public bathhouse, today this cafe is all industrial-chic decor and vintage furnishings; 2nd-floor balcony, too. *39 Yangmeizhu Xiejie,* 杨梅竹斜街39号

Berry Beans
16 D3

Meticulously fussy coffee at a *hutong* gem, formerly a Republican era brothel. The tiny roof terrace offers voyeuristic views. *7 Zhujia Hutong,* 朱家胡同7号

Neiliansheng Shoe Shop
STRIPPEDPIXEL.COM/SHUTTERSTOCK ©

Shopping

Souvenirs

Qiánkūn Kōngjiān
17 D2

A bit hit or miss, this boutique is worth a browse for its old prints, maps, fabrics and stele rubbings. *26 Yangmeizhu Xiejie,* 杨梅竹斜街26号

Neiliansheng Shoe Shop
18 E2

Treat your feet to hand-stitched cloth shoes from this Beijing shop dating to 1853. *34 Dashilar Jie,* 大栅栏街34号

Books

Page One
19 E1

Good selection of English-language novels and Lonely Planet guides at one of Beijing's best bookshops, a three-floor Singapore chain. *Bldg E11, East Block, Beijing Fun,* 北京坊东区E11号楼

Róngbǎozhāi
20 B2

Landscape paintings, calligraphy scrolls, woodblock prints and traditional art supplies. *19 Liulichang Xijie,* 琉璃厂西街19号

See p118
for eating
and drinking
listings

Explore
Sanlitun & Chaoyang

Modern Beijing unfurls its feathers in Sanlitun (三里屯), the premier destination for shopping, posing and partying until dawn. Out east beyond the old city walls, Sanlitun belongs to Chaoyang (朝阳), a district low on sights but not lacking in luxury hotels, gourmet eats, audacious urban architecture and, further afield, contemporary art at the 798 Art District. If you want a sense of how China envisions its future, this is the place to come.

Chaoyang district also hosts Beijing's ever-expanding central business district, 2.5km south of Sanlitun, where competing neon-lit skyscrapers climb into the clouds, including China Zun, the 10th-tallest building in the world. It's a great place to feast on global eats, be served a meal by a robot or plan a night out.

Getting Around

 Line 1
Runs east–west from central Beijing; stops at Yong'anli (Silk St) and Guomao (CITIC Tower, Line 10).

 Line 3
Projected to open by the end of 2024, the east–west line 3 will connect Dongsi Shitiao (line 2) with Workers' Stadium and Tuanjiehu (Taikoo Li).

🅢 **Line 6**
Runs east–west from central Beijing; stops at Chaoyangmen (Dongyue Temple, Line 2) and Hujialou (Line 10).

🅢 **Line 10**
Runs north–south through the central business district; stops at Tuanjiehu (Taikoo Li), Guomao and Panjiayuan (Panjiayuan Market).

Taikoo Li shopping mall (p115)
ZDL/SHUTTERSTOCK ©

★

THE BEST

ART GALLERIES
798 Art District (p112)

SPURIOUS ANTIQUES
Panjiayuan Market (p110)

TAOIST DIORAMAS
Dongyue Temple (p116)

UNDERGROUND CLUBBING
Zhao Dai (p116)

SHOPPING MALL
Taikoo Li Sanlitun (p115)

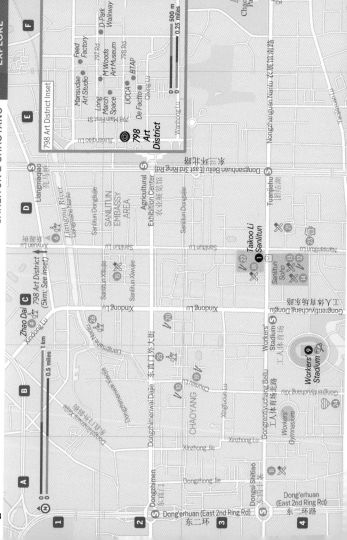

798 Art District Inset

798 Art District
798 Main First St

Mansudae Art Studio
Feed Factory
D-Park Walkway
797 Rd
797 Rd
798 Rd
M Woods Art Museum
Long March Space
UCCA
De Facto
BTAP
Qixing Lu

Jiuxianqiao Lu

Wanhong Lu

500 m
0.25 miles
0

Chaoyang Park

Nongzhanguan Nanlu 农展馆南路

Liangmaqiao 亮马桥

Xinyuan Lu

798 Art District (5km; See inset)

Zhao Dai

Xindong Lu

Dongsanhuan Beilu (East 3rd Ring Rd) 东三环北路

Liangma River
Liangmahe Nanlu
Liangmahe Nanlu

SANLITUN EMBASSY AREA

Agricultural Exhibition Center 农业展览馆

Tuanjiehu 团结湖

Tuanjiehu Lu

Sanlitun Lu

Taikoo Li Sanlitun

Sanlitun Xiliujie

Sanlitun Xiwujie

Sanlitun Lu

Sanlitun Lu

Sanlitun Soho

Nansanlitun Lu

Xindong Lu

Xindong Lu

Dongzhimenwai Dajie 东直门外大街

Gongti Lu 工体路

Gongrentiyuchang Donglu

Workers' Stadium 工人体育场

Workers' Stadium 工人体育场

CHAOYANG

Xingfu Lu

Xinzhong Lu

Gongrentiyuchang Beilu 工人体育场北路

Workers' Gymnasium 工人体育馆

Dongzhimen 东直门

Dongzhinerwai Dajie

Dongzhimenwai Xiejie

Dongsi Shitao 东四十条

Dongzhong Jie

Xinzhong Jie

Dongzhimen 东直门

Dong'erhuan (East 2nd Ring Rd) 东二环

Dong'erhuan (East 2nd Ring Rd) 东二环路

Dongzhong Jie

0   0.5 miles
0   1 km

N

For more see

⭐ Top Experiences p110
◯ Experiences p115
🍴 Eating p118
🍷 Drinking p119

Tuanjiehu Lu

Tuanjiehu Park

Chaoyang Beilu

Chaoyang Dajie

Hujialou Beijie

Chaoyang Dajie

CCTV Headquarters

Guanghua Lu 光华路

CITIC Tower

Panjiayuan Market 潘家园

Guomao 国贸

Dongsanhuan Zhonglu (East 3rd Ring Rd Middle) 东三环中路

Hujialou 呼家楼

Chaoyang Beilu

东大桥

Chaoyang Dajie

Guandongdian Nanjie

Jintaixizhao 金台夕照

Jintanlu Lu

Atmosphere

Jianguomenwai Dajie 建国门外大街

Jianguomenwai Dajie 建国门外大街

Dongdaqiao

Dongdaqiao Lu

Xiushui Dongjie

Dongdaqiao Lu

Yong'an Li 永安里

Xiushui Dongjie

Gongrentiyuchang Nanlu

Chaoyangmenwai Dajie 朝阳门外大街

Dongyue Temple 东岳

JIANGUOMENWAI EMBASSY AREA

DDC

DADA

Ritan Beilu

Ritan Park

Ritan Lu

Guanghua Lu 光华路

Xiushui Nanjie

Xiushui Beijie

Xiushui Dongjie 日坛东路

Ritan Donglu

Chaoyangmen 朝阳门

Chaoyangmenwai Dajie

Gongrenyuchang Nanlu

Yabao Lu

Ritan Lu

Dong'erhuan (East 2nd Ring Rd) 东二环

Jianguomen 建国门

Jianguomenwai Dajie 建国门外大街

Panjiayuan Market

A curio hunter's heaven or an Everest of fakery? Panjiayuan is both, and marvellous fun to boot. Picking over the wares of some 3000 dealers, you won't chance upon that priceless doucai stem cup, but you will find Mao busts, Little Red Books and faded cigarette posters.

MAP P108 **E8**

PLANNING TIPS

To get here, take subway line 10 to Panjiayuan, exit B, then head west on foot for 200m to find the main entrance. It's a big place, so budget two to three hours. It's open 8.30am to 6pm Monday to Friday, from 4.30am Saturday and Sunday.

Communist Kitsch

Panjiayuan (潘家园古玩市场, Pānjiāyuán Gǔwán Shìchǎng; 18 Huaweili, 华威里18号) is the place to pick up Mao memorabilia like the Little Red Book, a collection of his quotations brandished and recited by millions of Red Guards during the Cultural Revolution. With patience, you'll likely turn up a few English-language editions.

You can also find great propaganda posters ('Down with the American Imperialists!') and porcelain busts of the Great Helmsman among a variety of Mao pins and other Communist Party oddities.

Regardless of what you're buying, you can usually slash the initial asking price. Make a few rounds to compare prices before forking out, and bargain heartily. A good rule of thumb is to aim for a price based on how much you like the item, instead of whether or not it appears to be authentic.

Chinese Handicrafts

The market is a good place to look for Chinese calligraphy, scroll paintings, woodblock prints, seals and paper and inkstones. You can also buy replica Qing furniture, shards of smashed

Panjiayuan antique market
SIHASAKPRACHUM/SHUTTERSTOCK ©

porcelain from earlier dynasties, and thread-your-own bead necklaces. Note that you have a better chance of finding genuine antiques across town at Liulichang Culture Street, but expect stratospheric prices for the real thing.

Ghost Market

The market is at its biggest and best on weekends, starting well before dawn in the tradition of Qing dynasty *guǐ shì* (literally 'ghost markets'). Towards the beleaguered end of the dynasty, destitute nobles were forced to flog their family heirlooms and fineries, opting to do so under a face-saving veil of darkness. The present market was installed here in the early 1990s.

The earlier you arrive for the Ghost Market, the more chance you'll have of finding something unique.

TAKE A BREAK
A few stalls selling noodles are located at the edges of the market; you'll also find the usual international coffee chains.

EXPLORE

SANLITUN & CHAOYANG

798 Art District

The 798 Art District is an enclave of art galleries installed within a former 1950s factory complex. In the early noughties, Chinese artists turned the empty workshops into light-filled studios and saved it from destruction. 798 lost several major galleries during the pandemic, but is still worth exploring.

MAP P108 **E2**

PLANNING TIP
To get here, take subway line 14 to Wangjingnan, from where it's a 1.5km walk or a short cab ride to the south entrance. Most galleries are closed on Mondays.

Scan the QR code to access UCCA's website to see a list of the current exhibitions

Orientation

The **798 Art District** (798 艺术区, Qī Jiǔ Bā Yìshù Qū; cnr Jiuxianqiao Lu & 798 Lu, 酒仙桥路798路的路口) is an impressively large complex, making it hard for first-time visitors to know where to start. The best way to orient yourself is to find the **UCCA gallery** in the centre; from here, the core block where most of the other big galleries are located extends to the north. Wherever you go, keep an eye out for murals, graffiti, stencils, sculpture – 798 is a vibrant playground of public art and installations.

Architecture

The '718 Joint Factory', as 798 was originally known, was the gold standard of Communist industrial might in China from 1957 when it was built using materials imported from East Germany via the Trans-Siberian Railway all the way into the factory itself. Preservation orders saved the old factory station, tracks and a steam loco, along with giant industrial chimneys, workers' dorms and, most importantly, the light-filled Bauhaus factories and workshops. The scale of it all is bewildering, and it looks something like the ultimate steampunk movie set. For an elevated overview of this surviving slice of 1950s industrial China, walk the length of **D-Park Walkway** in the east of the complex.

798 entrance
RICK SIU/SHUTTERSTOCK ©

Galleries

Expect to pay an admission fee of around ¥60 for most of the big galleries.

UCCA

Remodelled in 2019, **UCCA** (Ullens Center for Contemporary Art; 尤伦斯当代艺术中心, Yóulúnsī Dāngdài Yìshù Zhōngxīn) remains the finest contemporary-art gallery in 798. Many global art superstars have made their China debuts here since it opened in 2007, and the gallery continues to stage boundary-pushing exhibitions – sometimes several at once, for which there is always an admission fee. UCCA was established by Belgian art collectors, who had purportedly amassed the world's largest collection of Chinese contemporary art. The couple sold the gallery to a group of Chinese investors in 2017 who, to the relief of the art world, opted to continue it as a nonprofit enterprise.

QUICK BREAK
For a proper meal, stop by the Sichuanese Feed Factory (吃厂, Chī Chǎng) in the north of the complex. Otherwise, you're never far from a cafe here.

BAUHAUS

A German modernist movement, Bauhaus architecture dictated that form should follow function. Communist regimes embraced elements of Bauhaus, particularly the emphasis on simplicity and inexpensive materials, but tended to ignore its aesthetic considerations.

DE FACTTO

Across from BTAP is **De Factto** (其实文化, Qíshí Wénhuà), a vinyl record shop, cafe and jazz venue. check out its WeChat account (defactto) for concert times.

Long March Space

A champion of emerging artists and the Chinese art scene generally since 2002, **Long March Space** (长征空间, Chángzhēng Kōngjiān) is one of 798's premier galleries for contemporary Chinese painting, sculpture and video installations.

M Woods Art Museum

Founded by Chinese art collectors in 2014, **M Woods** (木木美术馆, Mùmù Měishùguǎn) stages meticulously curated, themed art shows according to the gallery's founding principle of 'FAT' (Free, Alchemical, Timeless) – meaning that anything goes in terms of blending styles, genres and eras. The space is a thrilling maze of former factory spaces big and small over multiple floors.

BTAP

Associated with the Tokyo Gallery in Japan, **BTAP** (Beijing Tokyo Art Projects; 东京画廊, Dōngjīng Huàláng) was the first international gallery to lease space in 798 back in 2002. Since then, this modest Bauhaus factory workshop has staged the works of many a rising Chinese artist. Note the old Communist slogan on the brick wall across from the gallery: 'Uphold Mao Zedong thought'.

Mansudae Art Studio

An incongruous outpost of the Hermit Kingdom, **Mansudae** (万寿台创作社, Wànshòutái Chuàngzuò Shè) exhibits socialist-realist paintings and sculptures depicting soot-faced miners, chiselled soldiers and the lyrical landscapes of North Korea. The works are created by the official government studio in Pyongyang, responsible for all the public art and statuary in the country. You can also buy genuine DPRK souvenirs, including commemorative stamps and propaganda magazines with shiny tractors on the cover.

EXPERIENCES

See & Be Seen at Taikoo Li
MALL

MAP: **1** P108 **C4**

Beijing's premier destination for haute couture and urbane dining, **Taikoo Li** (三里屯太古里, Sānlítún Tàigǔlǐ; 19 Sanlitun Lu, 三里屯路19号) is where the fashionistas go to splash the cash. An open-air mall complex either side of Opposite House hotel, Taikoo Li North is the better-bred half, carrying luxe labels such as Alexander McQueen, Canada Goose and Korea's Gentle Monster eyewear, while down south is Apple, Adidas and most restaurants, the best of which have top-floor alfresco terrace seating.

The Underground Music Scene
LIVE MUSIC

In the Russian district of south Chaoyang are two of Beijing's longest-running music clubs: Dada and DDC. Both relocated from central Beijing in 2021, escaping the strict zoning laws and steep rents of the central *hutong*, to the abandoned basement of a grungy post-apocalyptic building.

DADA (MAP: **2** P108 **B6**; @dada barbeijing; B1, Block A, Ritan International Trade Center, 日坛国际贸易中心A座北门B1, 南营房胡同), accessed via the building's northwest entrance, is one of Beijing's premier venues for esoteric, bass-heavy beats, while remaining unpretentious and divey enough for the casual partygoer. By combining an imaginative lineup of DJs at weekends with its new industrial setting, Dada gets the underground party vibe spot on.

In the same underground complex on the northeast side is **DDC** (MAP: **3** P108 **B6** Dusk Dawn Club; @ddc_duskdawnclub; 黄昏黎明俱乐部, Huánghūn Límíng Jùlèbù; B1, 39 Shenlu Jie, 神路街39号地下一层), a good place to catch small and mid-sized bands, from post-rock noise outfits to folk strummers, both Chinese and international. It has a capacity of 700, and has a similar bomb-shelter aesthetic.

Check the Instagram accounts for both venues for the schedules.

 BLIND MASSAGE

The general idea behind Chinese massage (*tuīná*; 推拿) is that it stimulates the qi (energy) that flows along the body's meridians or pathways. Massage is not just about relieving tight muscles; it is also used to treat a variety of ailments. To receive a real-deal foot or body massage, consider a blind massage centre (search for 盲人按摩 on Dianping or Baidu Maps). If it's candlelight, aromatherapy and soothing music you're after, try a popular spa chain such as Dragonfly (dragonfly.net.cn) or Bodhi (bodhi.com.cn) instead.

Clubbing in Chaoyang
CLUBS

Beijing's largest bling-centric dance clubs are located on the west side of the Workers' Stadium, but for a more egalitarian night of dancing you'll have to venture into northern Chaoyang. Check out the **Safehouse Collective** (Bǎihuì; 百会; baihui.live), a local resource for electronic music.

Zhao Dai (MAP: ④ P108 **C1**; @zhaodaiclub; Zhāodàisuǒ, 招待所; Genasi Bldg, 19 Xinyuanli Xilu; 新源里西19号格纳斯大厦) is a reliable choice for techno, and has a large dance space northeast of Dongzhimen. **Groundless Factory** (MAP: ⑤ P108 **F4**; @groundlessfactory; Mòxūyǒu Gōngchǎng, 莫须有工厂; iWork Cultural & Creative Park, beneath the Water Tower, 5 Zuigongfen, 醉公坟甲5号, 安家iWork文创, 水塔下) has a warehouse space that can hold upwards of 1000 people and occasionally hosts big-name DJs. It's way out by the 5th Ring Rd, east of Chaoyang Park.

Finally, there's **Wigwam** (MAP: ⑥ P108 **D1**; @wigwam.live; 4 Jiangtai Shangye Jie, 将台商业街4号), which features a rotation of local DJs with the occasional big international name in a more intimate space. It's near the 798 Art District.

High Life
BAR

MAP: ⑦ P108 **D8**

For a view of some of Beijing's landmark modern buildings – notably the CCTV Headquarters (aka Big Pants) and the city's tallest skyscraper, the CITIC Tower – head up to the 80th-floor bar, **Atmosphere** (云酷, Yúnkù; China World Summit Wing, 1 Jianguomenwai Dajie, 建国门外大街1号北京国贸大酒店80层). On top of the China World Tower, this is as high as you can get in Beijing. The lounge side has better views, while the bar side is a bit more rowdy with karaoke in the evenings. Expect to pay ¥68 for a beer and ¥158 for a glass of wine or a cocktail. There's a food menu, too. It's open 2pm to 2am daily. Enter through the Shangri-La Hotel lobby, near the Guomao subway station.

Into the Mystic
TAOIST TEMPLE

MAP: ⑧ P108 **B5**

Dedicated to Tai Shan, the eastern peak of China's five Taoist mountains, the morbid **Dongyue Temple** (东岳庙, Dōngyuè Miào; 141 Chaoyangmenwai Dajie, 朝阳门外大街141号) is an unsettling, albeit fascinating place of worship. The unlit central halls evoke a gloomy yet genuine air of mysticism that's unlike any other shrine in Beijing.

One of the highlights is the series of macabre dioramas representing various bureaucratic departments from the Taoist underworld. Inside, you can muse on life's finalities by examining the various displays, some 76 in total, depicting such scenes as the Department for Wandering Ghosts or the Department for Implementing 15 Kinds of Violent Death.

TAOISM

Taoism (道教; Dàojiào; literally, the teachings of the Way) is the hardest Chinese religion to grasp. A natural counterpoint to Confucian hierarchy and order, much of its religious culture derives from ancient animism and shamanism. In everyday life, Taoism served several purposes, including self-cultivation and the transformation of inner energy (qi); the exorcism of evil spirits; divination; and rituals that secured blessings from the gods. Chinese medicine, martial arts and technology were all greatly influenced by Taoist practices. Taoism initially drew from the teachings of ancient philosophers such as Laozi (who wrote the 道德经 or Dao De Jing) and Zhuangzi. However, Chinese scholars tend to differentiate between Taoist philosophy and religion.

Other parts of the temple are no less fascinating. Cavernous Daiyue Hall is consecrated to the God of Tai Shan, who sits inside, managing the 18 layers of hell. Visit during festival time, especially during Chinese New Year and the Mid-Autumn Festival, and you'll see the temple at its most vibrant.

The back halls have been turned into a folk customs museum, where visitors will find displays of objects ranging from millstones to lacquerware to kites to stage jewellery for actors.

See a Match at Workers' Stadium

SPORT

MAP: **9** P108 **B4**

One of Mao's '10 Great Buildings' erected in 1959 to mark a decade of the People's Republic of China, the **Workers' Stadium** (工人体育场, Gōngrén Tǐyùchǎng; Gongrentiyuchang Beilu, 工人体育场北路) staged several Mass Games here during the early days, where thousands of athletes would move as one to spell out giant Chinese characters. The original building was demolished in 2020, making way for a new and improved Workers' Stadium in 2023 with a capacity of 68,000 spectators.

Football fans will relish the chance to see Guo'an, Beijing's local team, in action. Average attendance for a Guo'an home game is more than 40,000, and watching a match before hitting the Sanlitun bars and clubs guarantees a fun night out for football fans. It also gives everyone the opportunity to enhance their Chinese vocab with a few colourful local expressions!

The Chinese Super League has 16 teams; each team plays 30 matches between (roughly) March and November. International friendlies are also held at Workers' Stadium. Ticket sales are announced on the club's WeChat page and sold on Damai's WeChat platform.

EXPLORE

SANLITUN & CHAOYANG

Best Places for...

See page 108 for map of locations

❤ Budget   ❤❤ Midrange   ❤❤❤ Top End

Eating

Regional Chinese

Méizhōu Dōngpō Jiǔlóu
眉州东坡酒楼 ❤
10 B2

Great-value Sichuan classics alive with the tongue tingle of *huajiao* (Sichuan peppercorns) at this reliable neighbourhood favourite. *7 Chunxiu Lu,* 春秀路7号

Baron Rozi Uyghur Restaurant
巴依老爷 ❤
11 A4

Think faux-rococo, chandeliers and a cavernous dining hall: a delightful setting in which to gorge on Xinjiang *dapanji* (spicy chicken stew). *Xinzhong Bldg, Gongrentiyuchang Beilu,* 工人体育场北路新中大厦

Māmā de Wèidào
妈妈的味道 ❤
12 C4

Come to Mama's for the quiet setting and refined home cooking. From sweet-and-sour spare ribs to stir-fried eggs and tomatoes, you can't go wrong. *2nd fl, T+Mall, Nansanlitun Lu,* 南三里屯路通盛中心2楼

Chua Lam's Dim Sum
蔡澜港式点心 ❤❤
13 C4

Hawthorn barbecued pork buns, crystal shrimp dumplings and other dim-sum delicacies at this casual Hong Kong diner. *1st fl, T+Mall, Nansanlitun Lu,* 南三里屯路通盛中心1楼

Hǎidǐlāo 海底捞 ❤❤
14 C4

China's best-loved chain of spicy hotpot restaurants: order hand-pulled noodles for a tableside performance of warrior-like twirling. *Soho Mall Bldg 6, 8 Gongti Beilu,* 工体北路8号三里屯SOHO6号商场

Stylish Eats

In & Out 一坐一忘 ❤❤
15 C2

Take your taste buds to China's southwest at this sophisticated Yunnanese spot. Classic dishes like are gorgeously presented. *1 Sanlitun Beixiaojie,* 三里屯北小街1号

Crystal Jade
翡翠江南 ❤❤
16 D8

Superbly styled Shanghai dim sum like ultra-delicate, colourful *xiǎolóngbāo* (soup dumplings) at a Singapore icon. *4th fl, China World Mall, 1 Jianguomenwai Dajie,* 建国门外大街1号国贸商城4层

Country Kitchen
乡味小厨 ❤❤❤
17 D6

Treat yourself to roast lamb and Peking duck at the Rosewood Hotel's Michelin-starred northern Chinese restaurant. *3rd fl, Rosewood Hotel, Dongsanhuan,* 东三环呼家楼北京瑰丽酒店3层

Peking Duck

Taste of Dadong (Rhapsody) 小大董 ❤❤
18 C3

A cool blue colour scheme and some food theatre make this the city's best 'modern duck' experience. *3rd fl, Taikoo Li South*

Block, Sanlitun Lu, 三里屯路太古里南区3层

Jingzun Peking Duck
京尊烤鸭店
19 B3

An unsung purveyor of Peking duck, Jingzun's bargain birds (¥198/108 whole/half) are every bite the equal of Beijing's more elite brands. *6 Chunxiu Lu,* 春秀路6号

Shèng Yǒng Xīng
晟永лич烤鸭店 ❷❷❷
20 C2

High-roller Peking duck, roasted over jujube wood for a less-oily bite. *5 Xindong Lu,* 新东路5号

International

Taco Bar 塔科酒吧 ❷❷
21 D4

Taco Bar packs out with partiers feasting on Mexican street-style tacos and killer cocktails. *Lot 10, Courtyard 4, off Gongrentiyuchang Beilu,* 北京机电院内4号院

Migas Mercado
米家思 ❷❷
see **16** D8

Spanish-run Migas serves sun-drenched fare including grilled octopus and Iberian pork on a fabulous terrace in the CBD. *7th fl, China World Mall, 1 Jianguomenwai Dajie,* 建国门外大街1号 国贸商城三期北区7层

+Pink 越南料理 ❷❷
22 C3

Modern Vietnamese spot that plays all the classics: *phở, bánh mì,* spring rolls and iced coffee. *3rd fl, Taikoo Li South Block, Sanlitun Lu,* 三里屯路太古里南区3层

Home Plate BBQ
本垒美式烤肉 ❷❷
see **21** D4

Flying the American BBQ flag, this Texan-owned restaurant is all about slow-cooked meat, burgers and craft beer. *Lot 10, Courtyard 4, off Gongrentiyuchang Beilu,* 三里屯机电院10号

Tienstiens 将将 ❷❷
see **21** D4

Sophisticated, spacious rooftop cafe with French wines and cheese. *Lot 10, Courtyard 4, off Gongrentiyuchang Beilu,* 工人体育场北路4号 10号楼

Drinking

Bars

Slowboat Brewery
23 D4

Drop anchor at Slowboat, one of Beijing's original American-run craft brewers, for three floors of busy, beery fun. *6 Nansanlitun Lu,* 南三里屯路6号

Destination
24 B4

Beijing's best queer club has multiple rooms, an outdoor bar, a restaurant and a programme of LGBTIQ+ events. *bjdestination.com.cn, 7 Gongrentiyuchang Xilu,* 工体西路7号

Mei Bar
see **17** D6

Glamorous hotel bar with multiple rooms, an outdoor deck and respectable mixology. *5th fl, Rosewood Beijing, Dongsanhuan,* 东三环呼家楼北京瑰丽酒店5层

Paddy O'Shea's
25 B2

For that crucial match you can't miss, Paddy's is the place. Multiple screens. *28 Dongzhimenwai Dajie,* 东直门外大街28号

Arrow Factory Brewing
26 C1

Combines inventive craft ales with impeccable pub grub, served in a two-tiered building with a roof terrace facing the Liangma River. 亮马河南路, *Liangmahe Nanlu*

See p131
for eating
and drinking
listings

Explore
Summer Palace & Haidian

The sprawling Haidian District (海淀区, Hǎidiàn Qū) stretches as far as the Western Hills, which for centuries have offered an escape from the dust, heat and noise within the old city walls. It was here that the Summer Palace (Yiheyuan) was built, the principal survivor of a great swath of regal real estate encompassing the Old Summer Palace (Yuanmingyuan) and the temple-strewn peaks of the Fragrant Hills. Today, Haidian is most famous for its cluster of universities, which revolve around the commercial centre of studenty Wudaokou. Next door, Zhongguancun is Beijing's tech and innovation hub.

Getting Around

 Subway Line 4
Connects central Beijing with the Haidian District. Stops at the National Library (for the canal temples) and the Summer Palace's east and north gates. Transfer via lines 1, 2, 6 and 19.

 Subway Line 13
Runs from Xizhimen (line 2) to Wudaokou.

 Train
The Xijiao Line, a light railway, serves the Fragrant Hills, the Botanical Gardens and the Summer Palace's west gate. It connects with the subway at Baogou (line 10).

THE BEST

IMPERIAL GARDENS
Summer Palace (p124)

CANAL-SIDE PAGODA
Wuta Temple (p128)

AUTUMN SCENERY
Fragrant Hills (p130)

STUDENT NIGHTLIFE
Wudaokou (p129)

BUDDHIST STATUARY
Wanshou Temple (p128)

Summer Palace (p124)
PHOTO HEDGE/SHUTTERSTOCK ©

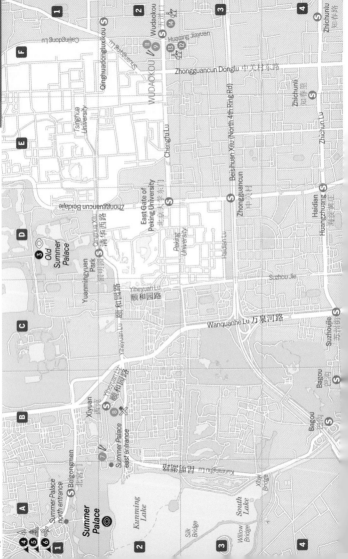

Cailingdong Lu

Qinghuadongluxikou S

Wudaokou 五道口

WUDAOKOU V

Huaqing Jiayuan

Tsinghua University

Zhongguancun Donglu 中关村东路

Chengfu Lu

Zhichunli 知春里

Zhongguancun Beidajie

East Gate of Peking University 北京大学东门

Beisihuan Xilu (North 4th Ring Rd)

Zhichun Lu 知春路

Old Summer Palace

Qinghua Xilu 清华西路

Peking University

Zhongguancun 中关村

Yuanmingyuan Park 圆明园

Haidian

Huangzhuang S 海淀黄庄

Yiheyuan Lu 颐和园路

Haidian Lu

Suzhou Jie

Wanquanhe Lu 万泉河路

Xiyuan 西苑

Yiheyuan Lu 颐和园路

Suzhoujie 苏州街 S

Bagou 巴沟 S

Baigongmen 北宫门

Summer Palace north entrance S

Summer Palace east entrance

Kunminghu Lu 昆明湖路

Summer Palace

Kunming Lake

South Lake

Silk Bridge

Willow Bridge

Xixi Bridge

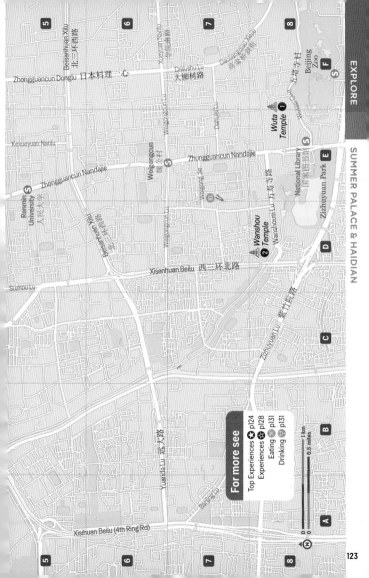

Beisanhuan Xilu 北三环西路

Zhongguancun Donglu 日本料理 一心

Xueyuan Nanlu 学院南路

Daliushu Lu 大柳树路

Gaoliangqiao Xijie 高粱桥斜街

Wutasi Cun 五塔寺村

Wuta Temple ❶

Beijing Zoo

Ⓕ Ⓢ

Kexueyuan Nanlu

Wangzhuang Lu

Dahui Lu

Weigongcun 魏公村 Ⓢ

Zhungguancun Nandajie

National Library 国家图书馆

Ⓔ

Rennin University 人民大学 Ⓢ

Zhongguancun Nandajie

Beisanhuan Zhonglu

Chengfu Lu

Weigong Jie

Weigongcun Lu

Wanshou Temple ❷

Wanshousi Lu 万寿寺路

Zizhiyuan Park

Ⓓ

Suzhou Lu

Xisanhuan Beilu 西三环北路

Zizhuyuan Lu 紫竹院路

Ⓒ

For more see

Top Experiences ⭐ p124
Experiences ⭐⭐ p128
Eating ✹ p131
Drinking ☕ p131

Yuanda Lu 远大路

Banjing Lu

Xisihuan Beilu (4th Ring Rd)

1 km
0.5 miles

Ⓐ Ⓑ

Ⓝ

Summer Palace

A marvel of imperial garden design and one of Beijing's must-see attractions, the Summer Palace (颐和园, Yíhéyuán) was the preferred residence of the Empress Dowager Cixi. It merits an entire day's exploration, although a few hours exploring its arched bridges, pavilions and hillside temples is a good place to start.

MAP P122 **A2**

PLANNING TIP
The main entrance is the East Palace Gate, near the Xiyuan subway station. Avoid backtracking by exiting through the north or west entrances, both of which have their own subway stations.

Scan this QR code to book tickets for the Summer Palace

History

The Summer Palace was part of the domain of imperial gardens long before the Qianlong Emperor embellished it as the Garden of Clear Ripples in the mid-18th century. The oldest surviving sections are its waterways – the central Kunming Lake was originally a reservoir dug during the Yuan dynasty for the city's water supply. However, today the palace is most famous as the favoured retreat of imperial China's last true ruler, the Empress Dowager Cixi.

Even as the **Old Summer Palace** (p129) has come to symbolise the transgressions of the foreign imperial powers, the existing Summer Palace has come to stand for Cixi's self-indulgent decadence and feudal misrule that stymied China's modernisation efforts. Cixi's court allegedly embezzled funds earmarked for the Chinese navy in order to help renovate the Summer Palace just before the disastrous Sino-Japanese War of 1895. China needed a modern navy, the story goes, but all it got was Cixi's marble boat.

After this defeat, the Guangxu Emperor, for whom Cixi had been ruling as regent, attempted to seize power and institute the sweeping 100 Days' Reform in 1898. Cixi responded by staging a coup and initially confining the emperor to a

EXPLORE

SUMMER PALACE & HAIDIAN

Kunming Lake
FRANK FELL MEDIA/SHUTTERSTOCK ©

single courtyard in the Summer Palace. He died
less than 24 hours before Cixi in 1908; most
believe he was poisoned.

Layout

The Summer Palace was built around the central
Kunming Lake, with the main sights – the
imperial residence and Longevity Hill – along the
northern banks. A ferry route runs from the east
shore to the northwestern shore; alternatively,
hiring your own boat at one of the jetties is a
great way to escape the crowds. Following the
West Causeway to the East Shore makes for a
great walking circuit with its lakeside views and
arched bridges, while the area behind Longevity
Hill has two unusual attractions.

Pick up an audio guide (¥40) at the entrance
for in-depth commentary.

QUICK BREAK
There are no
restaurants inside
the Summer
Palace grounds.
Bring your own
snacks and eat a
good breakfast at
Qingfeng Steamed
Dumplings (p131)
outside the east
gate before
entering.

THE MARBLE BOAT
The western limit of the Long Corridor opens onto Cixi's infamous marble 'boat', which has come to embody how out of touch with geopolitical reality China's late imperial rulers were.

Hall of Benevolence & Longevity

Entering via the East Palace Gate, visitors arrive at the **Hall of Benevolence & Longevity**, from where Cixi ran the government. Glimpse the grand throne within; the rockery outside was designed to mimic the famous Lion Grove Garden in Suzhou. Note also the dragon and phoenix statues in the courtyard, the symbolic embodiment of emperor and empress. Here it's the phoenix that commands centre spot, a clear sign that a woman was running the show. But it wasn't all work and no play. To the north is the three-storey **Grand Theatre** where the court would enjoy opera performances. Westwards are the living quarters, which still contain dusty Qing-era furniture. Be sure to track down the **Hall of Jade Waves**, where you can see the remains of the brick walls that Cixi erected in order to imprison the Guangxu Emperor here in 1898.

Hall of Benevolence & Longevity
JEJIM/SHUTTERSTOCK ©

The Long Corridor

Cixi's living quarters were perfectly placed for access to the **Long Corridor**, a canopied walkway zigzagging westwards for 728m along the north shore of Kunming Lake at the foot of Longevity Hill. One can easily imagine Cixi being carried here in her sedan chair, enjoying the cool breeze off the water and admiring the artwork painted on every crossbeam, column and ceiling arch.

Longevity Hill

The Summer Palace's most commanding landmark is the octagonal **Pagoda of Buddhist Incense**, which rises 41m above the slopes of Longevity Hill. On the summit, behind the pagoda, is the **Hall of the Sea of Wisdom**. Adorned with 1008 niche images of the Buddha, it's one of the loveliest buildings in the palace and has sensational views over Kunming Lake towards Beijing. At the foot of Longevity Hill is the **Hall of Dispelling Clouds**, built by the Qianlong Emperor for his mother on her 60th birthday.

West Causeway

The further west you venture in the Summer Palace, the lighter the crowds become. The slender **West Causeway** flows south for 2km over the water, crossing six bridges, the highlight being the remarkably steep **Jade Belt Bridge**. The willow-lined promenade offers some of the best spots to take photographs of the Summer Palace. If you don't have the energy to circumnavigate the whole park, you can exit at the West Gate for the Xijiao Line, or return to catch the ferry by the Marble Boat.

Behind Longevity Hill

Atop the northern end of Longevity Hill, the **Four Great Regions** are a cluster of Tibetan-style buildings that mark the start of the climb down to the North Palace Gate. At the base of the rear of the hill is **Suzhou Street**, where emperors and their consorts would pretend to be regular folk by shopping for trinkets, with eunuchs acting as shopkeepers.

EXPERIENCES

Admire Stone Carvings at the Wuta Temple   BUDDHIST TEMPLE

MAP: ❶ P122 F8

If any Beijing sight can vanquish the dreaded 'temple fatigue', it's **Wǔtǎ Sì** (五塔寺; 24 Wutasi Cun, 五塔寺村24号). This little-known gem is eminently worthy of a pilgrimage, not just for its remarkable design, which owes more to India than imperial China, but also for the magnificent scatter of ancient masonry – statues, stelae, altars and thrones – salvaged from ruins around Beijing.

Built in 1473 for a visiting Indian lama, Zhenjue Temple, as it was then called, was one of many temples that lined the canal linking the capital with the imperial gardens. Inspired by the Mahabodhi Temple in India, the boxlike Wuta is pockmarked on all four sides by hundreds of images of the Buddha, each with unique mudras (hand gestures). This temple was a particular favourite of the Qing rulers – the Qianlong Emperor threw two lavish birthday parties here for his mum and had a similar pagoda built at the Azure Clouds Temple (p130).

In lieu of its long-lost temple halls, the relatively empty grounds have been given over to the **Beijing Art Museum of Stone Carvings**, with many examples dating back to the Mongol Yuan dynasty and some as far back as the Eastern Han. It's east of the National Library subway station. The temple is closed on Mondays.

Visit the Tranquil Wanshou Temple   BUDDHIST TEMPLE

MAP: ❷ P122 D8

The tranquil, little-visited **Wanshou Temple** (万寿寺, Wànshòu Sì; 121 Wanshousi Lu, 万寿寺路121号) was originally consecrated for the storage of Buddhist texts in 1577. Today, it's

 AI IN THE CAPITAL

Haidian is home to dozens of universities, including two of China's finest: Peking University and Tsinghua University. But in recent years, the district has shot to fame thanks to Zhongguancun, China's Silicon Valley, fed by the talent pool of China's brightest young graduates. A thriving incubation district of start-ups, tech companies and innovation backed by government funding, Zhongguancun started out as a street selling consumer electronics in 1978 when China began its initial round of economic reforms. Zhongguancun has evolved to become China's artificial intelligence heartland, where over a dozen AI labs crunch reams of big data to develop emerging technologies like facial recognition, virtual assistants and chatbots that have been trained to toe the Party line.

more museum than a temple, with some excellent displays of antiques.

Walking beneath the magnolia trees in the opening courtyard and the temple history exhibits in the initial Hall of the Heavenly Kings takes visitors to a prized collection of bronze statuary in the second courtyard, which presents Chinese depictions of Sakyamuni, Manjusri, Amitabha and Guanyin in one side hall, balanced out with Tibetan figures in the wing opposite.

In the two-storey Wanshou Hall in the next courtyard is an excellent exhibit on the motif of longevity in painting, ceramics and woodcarving. This is followed by the Da Chan Hall, which has a display of calligraphy, ink stones and brushes. The pavilion at the rear of the complex holds a miniature Ming dynasty pagoda alloyed from gold, silver, zinc and lead, while next to this, in an adjacent courtyard, is a collection of Ming and Qing furniture.

The temple is west of the National Library subway station. It's closed on Mondays.

Bargain Beijing DRINKING

Beijing isn't the steal that it used to be, but you can still have a cheap night out in **Wudaokou** (五道口), the city's student hub. Raucous late-night Korean and Japanese restaurants serve inexpensive meals to the district's many students. 'The Wu' is also home to Beijing's cheapest bars and

clubs where a shot of something dubious might set you back just ¥10. A typical night out starts with Korean food and too much sochu (a Korean grain alcohol), and ends at Propaganda (p131), as divey a club as you could dare wish for.

Past Indignations at the Old Summer Palace PARK

MAP: **3** P122 **D1**

Shattered ruins are all that remain of the **Old Summer Palace** (圆明园, Yuánmíngyuán; 28 Qinghua Xilu, 清华西路28号), at one time the single most beautiful place in all imperial Beijing. Hundreds of Chinese and Tibetan-style buildings, in addition to several Jesuit-designed palaces, once dotted 350 hectares of exquisitely landscaped royal gardens to the city's northwest (for context, that's five times the size of the Forbidden City). But in what is surely one of the great cultural tragedies of the imperialist era, the entire compound was pillaged and then put to the torch by British and French troops in 1860. All that's left now is a public park.

While there is little here to see, the 'Garden of Perfection and Light' remains a singularly important place: its destruction has been forever inscribed in Chinese history books as a low point in the Middle Kingdom's humiliation by foreign powers. If you're interested in learning more about the events that led to the garden's pillaging, listen to the

HIKING AROUND BEIJING

If you want a real taste of that wild mountain landscape that lies beyond the 5th Ring Rd, it's best to join an organised hike.

While you could, in theory, piece together the public transport that gets you to some crumbling watchtower on the Great Wall, why make things difficult for yourself? Beijing Hikers (beijinghikers.com), in operation for over two decades, has already scouted all the best treks in the region, and provides hikers with a shuttle and local guide to get you there and back with minimum fuss.

There are usually multiple trips each week, with varying levels of distance and difficulty.

episode 'The Destruction of the Yuanmingyuan' from the podcast *Barbarians at the Gate*.

The former gardens cover a huge area – 2.5km from east to west – so be prepared for some walking, especially as the few marble ruins that remain, consisting of the Jesuit palaces and the Great Fountain, are far from the subway stop (Yuanmingyuan Park).

Leaf Peeping in the Fragrant Hills HIKING

A great swath of Beijing's Western Hills was once an imperial pleasure resort, acres of undulating pine-cypress forest peppered with temples, pavilions and lookouts dating to the Qing dynasty. Opened to the masses as a public park in 1956, **Fragrant Hills** (MAP: ❹ P122 A1; 香山公园, Xiāng Shān Gōngyuán; 40 Maimai Jie, 买卖街40号) is busiest in autumn when the maples are ablaze. On reasonably clear days you can see Beijing's skyscrapers, 20km distant, from Incense Burner Peak (557m). The superb Azure Clouds Temple is reason alone to visit.

For most visitors, Fragrant Hills Park is a thigh-burning ascent up zigzag lanes and endless steps, passing imperial villas and temples. Allow an hour from the main north entrance to Incense Burner Peak. Alternatively, take the chairlift to the peak, saving your energy for a long amble downhill.

Rather than making straight for the summit, start with a visit to the **Azure Clouds Temple** (MAP: ❺ P122 A1; 碧云寺, Bìyún Sì), just outside the park's main north entrance, with its five-towered pagoda and astonishing hall of 500 Buddhist luohan statues. Southwest of the temple is the enormous, Tibetan-style Temple of Brilliance, while nearby is Xiangshan's iconic Glazed Tile Pagoda.

Also nearby is the **Botanical Gardens** (MAP: ❻ P122 A1; 北京植物园, Běijīng Zhíwùyuán), which contain flower gardens, a greenhouse and the Sleeping Buddha Temple.

Best Places for...

① Budget **①①** Midrange **①①①** Top End

See page 122 for map of locations

Eating

Outside the Summer Palace

Qingfeng Steamed Dumplings
庆丰包子哺 **①**

7 B2

Outside the palace's east entrance, the steamed buns, noodles and dumplings at this popular chain make for a quick and tasty breakfast or lunch. *19 Gongmenqian Jie,* 宫门前街19号

Yúnhǎi Yáo 云海肴 **①①**

8 B2

Fabulous Yunnanese restaurant tucked away amid American fast-food chains at the Xiyuan subway station (the Summer Palace east entrance). *208 Yiheyuan Lu,* 颐和园路208号

Haidian District

Bāozhuāng Mǎchē
包装马车 **①**

9 F2

Sating homesick Koreans since 2004, this windowless eatery serves Seoul-style hotpots of rice cakes, tofu, instant ramen, veggies and a choice of protein. One pot is enough for two to three diners to share. *3rd fl, Dongyuan Plaza, 35 Chengfu Lu,* 成府路35号东源大厦3层

Golden Peacock 金孔雀德宏傣味餐馆 **①①**

10 E7

Yunnan favourites such as grilled fish with lemongrass and aromatic pineapple rice. The restaurant specialises in the cuisine of the Dai people. *1 Minzu Daxue Beilu, Weigongcun,* 魏公村民族大学北路1号楼1层

Isshin Japanese Restaurant
有薫一心日本料理 **①①**

11 F2

From maki rolls to beef hotpot, Isshin is a winner for Japanese food at student-friendly prices. It's set back from the main road, 150m northwest of Wudaokou station. *Room 403, West Bldg, 35-2 Chengfu Lu,* 成府路35-2号院内西楼403室

Drinking

Bars

Propaganda

12 F3

Propaganda is a long-established Wudaokou dive club with preposterously cheap drinks and cheesy EDM. *12 Huaqing Jiayuan,* 华清嘉园12号楼

Lush

13 F2

By day, Lush dishes up breakfast, burgers and salads at student-friendly prices. After dark, the beers and cocktails start flowing. *1 Huaqing Jiayuan, Chengfu Lu,* 华清嘉园1号楼2层

Wu Club

14 F2

Bargain drinks, pre-mixed EDM bangers and a hands-in-the-air college crowd bring the good times to this club beneath the U-Centre mall. *36 Chengfu Lu,* 成府路36号五道口购物中心一层

The Great Wall of China

The Great Wall of China is one of the most awe-inspiring monuments in the world, stretching thousands of kilometers across the empire's historic frontier. The most famous sections are easy to access from Beijing, drawing millions each year with their restored architecture and thoughtful amenities.

PLANNING TIP

Make arrangements as soon as you can. Badaling sets a daily limit of 65,000 visitors and holidays are especially busy. Mutianyu tours may also sell out.

Scan this QR code to book admission to Badaling's Great Wall and cable cars

Badaling

Badaling (八达岭, Bādálǐng) is the bedrock of Great Wall tourism and the government has laboriously restored its masonry since the 1950s. When Western travellers say they have seen the Great Wall, they usually mean Badaling. Group tours are easy to arrange and travellers may enjoy door-to-door service and knowledgeable guides. Yet Badaling is also a prime destination for solo travellers, as the bullet train from Beijing makes this park a cinch to visit on your own. The crowds can be intense, but Badaling's convenient location and heart-stopping views make it one of the most coveted day trips in the world. Entrance to the Great Wall is ¥40 for adults and free for seniors and children under six.

The architecture reflects Badaling's 16th-century heyday, but fortifications have existed here since the Warring States Period, more than 2000 years ago. The wall was designed with a width of 4–5m, which was said to fit 10 men standing abreast, and cavalrymen could ride horses from tower to tower. Badaling occupied a critical strategic position, especially when nearby Beijing became the Ming dynasty's capital in 1421.

Watchtower, Badaling section
VADIM PETRAKOV/SHUTTERSTOCK ©

Visit the Great Wall Museum

The Great Wall Museum, displaying more than 2000 artefacts, opened in 1994 to help visitors understand Badaling's history and importance. After a lull in attendance, the museum is currently being rebuilt and is expected to reopen sometime in 2025. The new design will see the museum expanded and modernised, and curators are actively enriching the collection.

Hike the Badaling Wall

This section of the Great Wall extends 12km over the Badaling highlands, connecting 43 watchtowers and undulating far beyond view. Yet the walkable part of Badaling is a manageable 3.74km, and visitors can pass through up to 19 watchtowers. The crenellations are high on both

TAKE A BREAK
The many watchtowers once served as lookout points and bases for signal fires. Today, the towers are handy enclosures for resting your legs or sheltering from the elements.

GEAR UP

The Great Wall is a demanding hike – prepare for rain, extreme temperatures and dense crowds. Despite the restoration, the steep stone walkways can challenge any visitor, and sturdy shoes are always a smart idea. Bags are allowed, so bring provisions such as water and snacks.

sides, so there's little danger of falling, and guards will stop visitors from climbing around. Tourists flood the wall all day long, and it's normal to stand shoulder-to-shoulder with hundreds of tourists as you inch your way down the brick floors.

The views are spectacular on both sides of the wall, and panoramic photos are easy to take on a clear day, as long as you manage to dodge all the selfie sticks. Inside the towers you can peer through windows and arrow slits, taking in the same vistas that archers surveyed during the Ming dynasty.

Ride the Badaling Cable Car

Badaling's cable car system is designed to suspend visitors over the ridges and deposit

Badaling cable car
ZVONIMIR ATLETIC/SHUTTERSTOCK ©

them at the summits. The transparent walls provide 360-degree views as you rise over the precipitous slopes. There are two well-marked cableways: the North Cableway is longer and adjacent to the main parking lot, while the South Cableway is shorter and a slightly longer walk from the bus or train. The cable cars are great for aerial shots of the wall, and they provide shortcuts for starting or ending a hike, taking only a few minutes from station to station. Alternatively, you can try the 'pulley' system: climb into a plastic chair and ride for 10 minutes up a narrow-gauge track, much like a rollercoaster.

Cable cars and pulley rides cost extra; including Great Wall admission, round-trip prices range from ¥100 to ¥180, though children six and under can ride the cable car for free. QR codes are posted on walls so you can purchase tickets using a smartphone. A well-marked ticket booth is also stationed at the cableways' base.

Shop the Market

A sloped road leads from the parking lot to the main entrance, and its pavements are lined with souvenir shops, cafes and restaurants. Life-size statues, sculpted to look like Ming dynasty workers and warriors, are scattered along the route.

The shopkeepers are easygoing for such a well-trafficked destination, although popular items like T-shirts and mugs can be found for a cheaper price back in Beijing. If you're travelling light, these shops are a smart place to stock up on food and bottled water.

The street has two sizeable public toilets, and you're wise to use one before venturing onto the wall.

TRY THE TRAIN
If you want to avoid Badaling tour operators, the bullet train from Beijing is a fast and economical option. The ride from Qinghe Railway Station (清河站, Qīnghé zhàn) takes less than 30 minutes, and the Badaling station is a quick walk from the park's main entrance. A few trains also run from Beijing North Station (北京北站, Běijīngběi Zhàn).

CAMERAS YES, DRONES NO
Photography is heartily encouraged, and you can take pictures anywhere in the park, but drones are strictly forbidden.

 **WALKING TOUR**

Explore Badaling

The Great Wall is the main attraction at Badaling, and these well-patrolled ramparts were designed for walking. When you've experienced this ancient wonder, you may also spend a few hours strolling the grounds of Badaling National Forest Park, a hub of hardy food and public art.

START	END	LENGTH
Badaling Railroad Station	Great Wall Museum	2.5km; three hours

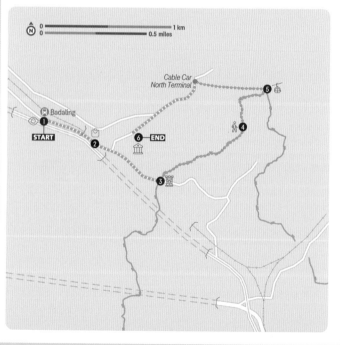

❶ Badaling Railway Station

Step off the train at the **Badaling Railroad Station** and take the escalator to street level. If you haven't already bought a return ticket, you can get one at the ticket booth located on the outside of the station. You can probably follow a crowd down the long car park to Badaling's shopping district. For this route, stop at the cableway window and buy a return ticket.

❷ Commercial Strip

Follow the road up to Badaling's main gatehouse. This route is a gauntlet of shops and eateries, where you can stock up on supplies before your hike or replenish after. Near the **gatehouse** is a food hall with several eateries inside, which can serve up a quick lunch later on. The wall has no toilets, so consider using a free one here.

❸ Fortified Entrance

An old fort serves as the **entrance to the Great Wall**, and you'll find a central plaza with long queues of visitors waiting to pass through. Head to the booths at the right of the entrance to secure your ticket. Advance reservations are highly recommended, and you can use the QR code on your receipt to receive a paper ticket.

❹ The Northern Section

Hike the northern section of the Great Wall, which will gradually lead you higher into the mountains. This popular route takes you through **several watchtowers**, and on a clear day you can see miles of undulating terrain. Crowds are common and exits are only for emergencies, so budget a good amount of time.

❺ Ride Back Down

You'll find the **North Cableway Station** at Tower 8. Use your ticket at the turnstile and take the walkway to the platform; an operator will help you into the cable car from there. Whether you're travelling alone or with company, the cable car can fit up to six passengers.

❻ Browse the Museum

Now that you've touched the Great Wall, learn about the people who built and defended this military masterpiece. When the **Great Wall Museum** reopens in 2025, state-of-the-art exhibits will tell the story of Emperor Qin Shi Huang and his 2200-year legacy.

TAKE THE TOBOGGAN DOWN

Mutianyu's 'toboggan' is a small plastic sled that follows a steel chute down the mountain. Adult riders can descend on their own or take a small child with them. The ride takes about five minutes and only goes downward, but the 10km speeds feel a lot faster when you're careening around the curves. You can accelerate or brake with a simple joystick. Head to Number 6 Watchtower and wait for the operator to tell you when to go; gravity will handle the rest. The toboggan has no established weight limit. Tickets cost ¥100 to ¥140 and can be purchased on-site.

Mutianyu

Northeast of Beijing, Mutianyu (慕田峪, Mùtiányù) is the second most popular section of the Great Wall, and it has much of the same appeal as Badaling: immaculate preservation, long hikes and dazzling views. The history also parallels Badaling, with most of the surviving construction dating back to the 16th century. Mutianyu is harder to reach by public transport and most travellers resort to charter buses. However, Mutianyu attracts a fraction of the traffic and, even in the high season, you may have entire towers to yourself.

Park admission is usually bundled into the price of a group tour – along with other perks – but if you travel to Mutianyu on your own, admission to the Great Wall is ¥40 for adults and free for seniors and children under six.

Shop and Eat at Mutianyu

A sizeable retail village is nestled at the foot of the mountains, where visitors can browse souvenir shops or pick from a range of restaurants. This lower section stands about 3km down the road from the cable-car stations, requiring most visitors to take a taxi or bus to the actual park entrance. The restaurants get fancier as you go higher up, and many of the shopfronts are tied to specific tour operators. Touts also hawk water and snacks – for inflated prices – on the wall itself, which can be a lifesaver on hot summer days.

Hike the Whole Way or Just Part

Visitors can walk about 5.4km of the Mutianyu Great Wall, which strings together 22 watchtowers and overlooks forested peaks and valleys. The wall's inclines vary from steep to very steep, and hikers should budget several hours to explore its full length. You may also consider hiking a smaller section of the wall, using the cable car, chair lift or toboggan to begin and end your walk.

Toboggan run
SIHASAKPRACHUM/SHUTTERSTOCK ©

If you really need to stretch your legs, there are two wooded trails that lead from the parking lot to the wall. These paved switchbacks terminate in the middle of the Mutianyu wall, at Towers 6, 8 and 10.

Mutianyu Cable Car or Chair Lift

The cable car is an enclosed capsule that carries up to six people up or down the mountain, depositing riders at the Number 14 Watchtower. Passengers can watch the scenery scroll by from all directions via the cable car's generous windows. If you're looking for a more open-air experience, the chair lift seats two and is exactly the model you'd find at a ski resort, carrying passengers back and forth from the Number 6 Watchtower. You can mix and match rides as much as you like, hiking on foot from one station to the other.

Tickets are usually purchased separately, even on group tours. Cable-car and chair-lift rides cost ¥100 for a one-way ticket and ¥140 round-trip.

Universal Beijing Resort

As throngs of excited parkgoers in their finest Hogwarts attire hurry past the spinning Universal globe, a sweeping melody rises to a crescendo – and so the Hollywood spell begins. They're all on their way to the capital's awesomest theme park: Universal Beijing Resort (北京环球度假区, Běijīng Huánqiú Dùjiàqū).

PLANNING TIP
In order to buy tickets, download the Universal Beijing Resort app. If you can't get the verification process to work overseas, try going through klook.com instead.

Scan this QR code to download the Universal Beijing Resort app

Rides

Universal Beijing is mid-sized as far as theme parks go – you should be able to hit all the main rides in one long day. There are five main lands, two of which are for younger kids (Minions, Kung Fu Panda) and three for everyone else (Harry Potter, Transformers and Jurassic World). Each land has three main rides.

The main attraction will always be the stunningly recreated crooked chimneys of Hogsmeade, where wizards from around the world stock up on wands, stage photoshoots at the train station and mount their broomsticks for the incredible 3D **Harry Potter and the Forbidden Journey**® – definitely not an experience for those with motion sickness.

The Transformers Metrobase has the biggest and baddest scream machine, the **Decepticoaster**, while the mellower **Jurassic Flyers** lets you imagine life as a pteranodon as you glide above the Isla Nublar's twin peaks and waterfall.

There is also Hollywood, which has a fun and little-visited film set (Lights, Camera, Action!), and the Waterworld Stunt Show, which is staged several times a day. Look out for shows at other venues throughout the day, like *Sing*.

Universal globe
TESTING/SHUTTERSTOCK ©

Practicalities

Like theme parks everywhere, you should expect long lines. If you're coming to Beijing specifically for Universal Studios, then consider staying at the resort – this gets you into the park one hour ahead of everyone else. Alternatively, buy Express tickets, which give you access to the VIP line. They are sold in packs of one, three or five rides, or you could opt for the entire park.

The rides are open 10am to 8pm weekdays, and 9am to 8pm weekends and holidays. Come early and expect to queue at the entrance, or arrive late – many visitors leave after the 5pm parade. Note that you do not get a ticket. Instead, you have to present your passport and do a facial recognition scan.

To get here, take subway lines 1 or 7 to the end of the line; it's an hour from the city centre. Children under 16 must be accompanied by an adult.

TAKE A BREAK
Every type of restaurant – from noodles to burgers and a chocolate emporium to roast duck – are located in the themed lands and on the City Walk that leads to the resort.

141

Beijing Toolkit

Shared bikes (p151)

TAREK ISLAM/SHUTTERSTOCK ©

Family Travel

The Chinese have a deep and uncomplicated love of children. Beijing may have fewer child-friendly facilities than equivalent-sized cities elsewhere, but the locals will go out of their way to accommodate kids.

Playgrounds

Toddlers will love running around Beijing's parks and squares, exploring their pathways and dancing along with the pensioners. Beihai Park (which has boats) and Jingshan Park are good choices. There are not many outdoor playgrounds, however (perhaps because of air pollution); for this type of fun you'll need to head indoors to a mall, where you pay for access.

WATERPARKS

Beijing in summer is hot – cool off on local water slides like those at the **Water Cube**, which hosted events at the 2008 and 2022 Olympics and is now also home to the city's largest waterpark.

Top Experiences

Beijing's top two sights for older kids are the **Great Wall** (p132) and **Universal Studios** (p140; pictured right). Mutianyu (Great Wall) is a good choice for families: it has a cable car, a toboggan ride and less-developed wilder sections of the Wall for explorers.

Universal Studios has a daily parade and mellower rides in the Kung Fu Panda and Minion lands that will appeal to younger kids; teens have plenty of thrilling rides to choose from.

Admission Prices

Kids can often get in for half price, or free if they are under 1.2m tall. It's always worth asking at the ticket office.

Getting Lost

Always arm your kids with a copy of your hotel's business card in case you get separated.

Dining

Dishes at Chinese restaurants are typically large and designed for sharing, and simple staples like plain cooked rice only cost a few yuan. If chopsticks are proving tricky, ask for a spoon (*sháozi*, 勺子).

Accommodation

Beijing has a number of fabulous luxury hotels, and you'll get a lot for your money compared to other world capitals.

Where to Stay if You Love...

 ### Authentic Alleyways
Drum Tower (p58) A great neighbourhood to experience local life in the capital, it's north of the Forbidden City and generally has good transport options. Look for midrange courtyard hotels in local *hutong*.

OUR PICK

★

We love to stay in...

Forbidden City & Dongcheng (p31) Not only is it convenient, this central area also has the widest range of accommodation. Wangfujing, east of the Forbidden City, has a number of five-star properties, but we prefer the traditional *hutong* around the Dongsi and Zhangzizhong Lu subway stations for a genuine taste of everyday Beijing life.

 ### The High Life
Sanlitun & Chaoyang (p107) Beijing's business district is also the buzziest once the sun sets. Skyscraping luxury hotels are relatively affordable and close to the city's hippest restaurants and bars.

HOW MUCH FOR A NIGHT IN A...

budget hotel **from ¥400**

boutique midrange **from ¥800**

luxury hotel **from ¥1600**

Online Booking
Trip.com is the most reliable site to book hotels for a Beijing stay and is the most likely to have up-to-date information. International booking sites do work, but may not have a full selection.

 ### Government Restrictions
Not all hotels in China are open to foreigners. Policies change constantly, so always double-check that a property has recent online reviews from foreign guests.

 ### Hostels & Flat Shares
Due to local laws, renting a room or apartment in Beijing is off-limits to tourists. Hostels are almost nonexistent following a bunk-bed ban aimed at migrant workers.

Food, Drink & Nightlife

⚠ Allergies & Intolerances

Peanuts, sesame and seafood are common ingredients. Wheat noodles are a Beijing staple, though rice is easy to find. Soy sauce and black vinegar are ubiquitous and contain gluten, as do vegetarian dishes (seitan).

HOW TO SAY

I'm allergic to... 我对 X 过敏　*Wǒ duì X guòmǐn*
peanuts 花生　*huāshēng*
sesame 芝麻　*zhīma*
seafood 海鲜　*hǎixiān*
gluten 面筋　*miànjīn*
vinegar 醋　*cù*
soy sauce 酱油　*jiàngyóu*

? ORDERING STRATEGIES

No English menu? One way to order is to look at what other diners are eating, point with a finger, and say, 'I want that' (*wǒyào nàgè*, 我要那个).

RESERVATIONS

Few places in Beijing take reservations; the secret to getting a table is to show up early and be prepared to wait. The queuing system is digital and requires a local phone number; if you don't have one, the hostess will try to accommodate you (eg by using her phone number).

🍽 Vegetarians

To say 'I am a vegetarian' in Chinese, the phrase is '*wǒ chī sù*' (我吃素). Traditional vegetarian restaurants are often near temples, and serve 'mock-meat' fare made from tofu, wheat gluten, mushrooms and vegetables. For other vegetarian options, look for international cafes and restaurants.

HOW TO... Pay the Bill

Going Digital Many restaurants in Beijing are fully digital. Putting your name on the waitlist, consulting a menu, placing an order and paying the bill is all done thorough your phone. While this is all quite convenient for Chinese speakers with a local phone number, most foreign tourists will need waitstaff to carry out the process for them. Beijingers realise that foreigners are usually helpless and are happy to lend a hand, so long as the restaurant is not crazy busy. The catch is that the entire process may be in Chinese only.

Cash A few places still have helpful picture menus; all will accept cash payments.

Tipping No one tips.

PRICE RANGES

The following price ranges refer to the cost of a meal for one person.

¥ less than ¥70

¥¥ ¥70–140

¥¥¥ more than ¥140

OPENING HOURS

Restaurants 10.30am to 2pm & 5pm to 10pm

Cafes 9am to 9pm

Bars 6pm to 2am

🥂 Going Out

Hutong Bars The haunt of hidden-gem cocktail dens and boho cafes, Beijing's *hutong*, especially around the Drum Tower, have broken away as a nightlife alternative.

Craft Beer Beer is China's most popular drink, and craft breweries have been on the rise in the past decade. Popular names include Great Leap, Slowboat, Jing-A, N Beer and Arrow Factory Brewing (pictured).

Live Music The *hutong* in the Drum Tower area have a handful of intimate live-music venues; the lakes of Beihai is a more boisterous area, with less discerning performances.

Karaoke (KTV) Hugely popular in China. Beijing has plenty of places where you can rent a windowless room to warble songs with friends, and have drinks and fruit brought in.

Dancing Clubland means the Workers' Stadium, where crazy-rich Beijingers roll up in Ferraris and bottles of champagne are expected. For more music-centric clubs, check out underground venues like Zhao Dai, Dada and Groundless Factory.

HOW MUCH FOR A...

order of dumplings
¥26

bowl of noodles
¥30

typical vegetable dish
¥35

typical meat dish
¥60

roast duck
¥238

local beer
¥10

coffee
¥35

craft beer
¥60

LGBTIQ+ Travellers

The Chinese government's attitude towards the LGBTIQ+ community is: 'We won't bother you, so long as you stay in the closet'.

The Party Line

Although the government's attitudes to homosexuality have come a long way (it was officially classified as a mental disorder until 2001), the CCP has reversed course in recent years as the current regime has decided to zero in on traditional family values, with an emphasis on encouraging couples to have more children. Following these decisions, Beijing's LGBT Center, the largest in the country, closed in 2023; it's generally understood that the government decided to shut it down.

The Party has also banned the depiction of gay people (along with drinking and reincarnation) on television; in 2021 the ban was extended to effeminate men, with the official statement instructing broadcasters to 'resolutely put an end to sissy men and other abnormal aesthetics'.

Social Acceptance

Even with recent government crackdowns, Beijing still has a welcoming LGBTIQ community. Generally speaking, many Chinese are accepting of gays and lesbians so long as it does not involve their own family members or interfere with having children. Many young Beijingers hold similarly tolerant views as their peers elsewhere in the world.

DATING & NETWORKING APPS

Certain networking and dating apps are online in China, but your data is definitely not private. For men, Grindr sometimes works. For women, check out Lespark and The L.

——— LEGALITY ———

It's important to note that homosexuality is perfectly legal in China. There is no risk to travelling as a same-sex couple.

Resources

Destination (p119; bjdestination.com.cn) In Chaoyang, this is Beijing's longest-running queer club. It hosts guest DJs, organises cultural and arts events, and has an attached restaurant • **Utopia** (utopia-asia.com) An informative and occasionally updated guide to LGBTIQ+ hot spots in Beijing.

Health & Safe Travel

The upside to an authoritarian police state is that Beijing is incredibly safe: your greatest risk will likely be crossing the street.

AIR POLLUTION

Despite Beijing's reputation for dangerous air-pollution levels, the situation has improved and should continue to trend in a positive direction. Nevertheless, pollution levels often register as 'Unhealthy'. Travellers with chronic respiratory conditions should check the air-quality index (aqicn.org) before their trip.

The Police State

Police, soldiers and surveillance cameras are everywhere, and the consequences of engaging in illicit activity can be severe. This not only includes obvious no-nos (drugs, prostitution) but also any sort of political or religious activity – leave the 'Liberate Hong Kong' T-shirt at home and remember that anything you do or say online can potentially be traced to your physical location. While the government is primarily concerned with Chinese citizens, laws can be applied arbitrarily and courts do not rule in favour of foreigners.

— TAP WATER —

Do not drink tap water. Bottled water, soft drinks, alcohol and drinks made from boiled water (tea, coffee) are fine.

QUICK INFO

Crime

While rare, if you discover something has been stolen, report it immediately to the nearest Foreign Affairs Branch of the Public Security Bureau (PSB).

Hospitals

Beijing has a number of excellent international hospitals and clinics, most of which are in Chaoyang.

Pharmacies

Pharmacies (yàodiàn; 药店) are identified by a green cross and often stock Chinese and western medicine.

Road Safety

The greatest hazard in Beijing really is crossing the road. Traffic comes from all directions; bicycles and electric scooters, in particular, frequently ride the wrong way down streets and on sidewalks, and you can't hear them coming. Likewise, do not assume that vehicles will stop when the light turns red. Keep your head on a swivel and remember that pedestrians command no respect.

Responsible Travel

Follow these tips to leave a lighter footprint, support local and have a positive impact on communities.

Mitigation Versus Adaptation

'Green' is the new buzzword in China, and even the most skeptical visitors to Beijing have to acknowledge the improved air quality and vast numbers of hybrid and electric vehicles. While the Chinese government's dual carbon goal – to achieve peak CO_2 emissions by 2030 and carbon neutrality by 2060 – dominates the headlines, the real focus is less on mitigation (reducing CO_2 output) and more on adapting to a warming world.

Tourism

Tourism in China accounts for about 7% of the country's carbon emissions. According to a McKinsey study, accommodation is tourism's leading carbon emitter (60%), while transport, particularly air travel, accounts for 38% of emissions.

OUR PICK

★

Green Hotels

The most ecofriendly hotels in Beijing, like Hotel Éclat (eclathotels.com), are generally in the luxury category, as these customers are more willing to pay for the added costs.

Water Scarcity

While emissions are a concern, more emphasis is being placed on water security in northern China. The most ambitious water engineering project in human history is the incomplete South–North Water Transfer Project, which connects China's four main rivers via three separate canals, and has already brought 53 billion cubic metres of water to the parched north during its first phase.

Recycling

While Beijing trialled household recycling programmes during COVID-19, recycling bins are still treated as regular rubbish bins.

BIKE SHARE

Making use of the bike-share system (p67) is a great way to get around. Bike lanes are ubiquitous, wide and generally completely separate from car traffic. Additionally, Beijing's flat landscape makes pedalling a breeze.

Hybrid & Electric Vehicles

It's estimated that roughly half of all EVs worldwide are on China's roads, and Beijing is certainly among the world leaders when it comes to EV and hybrid vehicle adoption. Municipal regulations require all city taxis (approximately 66,000) to transition to either an EV or hybrid car by the end of 2025.

Likewise, Beijing already had 11,000 electric city buses in 2020, accounting for over 60% of its fleet. If you're wondering where all these vehicles charge, the capital has also pioneered battery swap stations, where taxis and private cars can install a fully charged battery in minutes.

RENEWABLE ENERGY

China has made impressive strides in the renewable energy sector. In 2022 it installed as much solar energy as the rest of the world combined, and in 2024 broke ground on a 6GW wind-and-solar project that will provide power to Beijing.

Climate Change & Travel

It's impossible to ignore the impact we have when travelling, and the importance of making changes where we can. Lonely Planet urges all travellers to engage with their travel carbon footprint. Many airlines and booking sites offer travellers the option of offsetting the impact of greenhouse gas emissions by contributing to climate-friendly initiatives around the world.

There are many carbon calculators online that allow travellers to estimate the carbon emissions generated by their journey; try **resurgence. org** using the QR code, right.

Accessible Travel

 ## Overview

Beijing has made an effort in recent years to update building codes and improve accessibility for those with mobility issues. However, implementation has been uneven and facilities are not always maintained. The best advice when travelling to China is to join a specialist tour that can fully cater to your needs.

Taxis & Buses

Accessible taxis were once present in Beijing; however, these have since been discontinued. Increasing numbers of city buses, in contrast, do have a wheelchair ramp at the rear door; these may be the simplest way of getting around.

Subway

While escalators in subways normally only go up, wheelchair lifts have been installed in numerous stations. However, you may have to find a staff member to operate them. There is no comprehensive list of barrier-free stations.

STREET LEVEL

If you're wheelchair-bound or have mobility issues, Beijing can be a major obstacle course. Sidewalks are often uneven and in a dangerous condition, with high curbs preventing wheelchair access. Many streets can be crossed only via underground or overhead walkways with steps. Bike lanes are more navigable than sidewalks, though they are chaotic and not without risks. Getting around the big sights has improved, but is still challenging in places. Consider taking a collapsible lightweight chair.

HOTELS

Staying at a top-end international chain is recommended, though reach out to the hotel in advance to find out what sort of facilities are really in place. Few Chinese hotels have roll-in showers.

TOILETS

Accessible toilets can be found at major sights, top-end hotels and shopping malls, but squat loos elsewhere, including restaurants and fast-food chains, definitely present a challenge. Come prepared.

Resources

easytourchina.com
Two tours designed specifically for those with mobility issues.

⬡ Nuts & Bolts

🕐 Opening Hours

Officially, China has a five-day (Monday to Friday), 40-hour work week. In reality, many business practice the 996 work week, meaning employees work 9am to 9pm for six days. Most major tourist sights close on Mondays.

Banks 9am–5pm Monday to Friday, some open weekends

Bars 6pm–2am

Cafes 9am–9pm

Museums & Temples 8.30am–4.30pm Tuesday to Sunday

Parks 6am–9pm, shorter hours in winter

Restaurants 10.30am–2pm, 5–10pm

Shops 10am–9pm

> **QUICK INFO**
>
> **Time zone**
> China Standard Time (GMT/UTC plus eight hours)
>
> **City code**
> +010
>
> **Emergency number**
> 120
>
> **Population**
> 21.9 million

🚻 Toilets

Generally, toilets at major tourist sights will have seated options, while public WCs in smaller *hutong* are still squat loos with minimal privacy. Toilet paper is often provided in Beijing (it's by the sink, not the stall), but keep a stash on you just in case. Throw it in the waste bin, not the toilet.

📅 Public Holidays

China has seven official public holidays. It's not a great idea to arrive in China or go travelling during the big holiday periods (Chinese New Year and National Day) as hotel prices reach their maximum and transport can become impossible.

New Year's Day
1 January

Chinese New Year
January or February (a weeklong holiday for most)

Tomb Sweeping Day
4 or 5 April

International Labour Day
1 May

Dragon Boat Festival
June (one day)

Mid-Autumn Festival
end of September (one day)

National Day
1 October (a weeklong holiday for most)

ELECTRICITY
120V/60Hz, 230V/50Hz

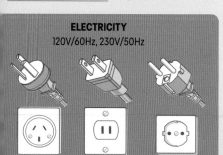

Open
kāimén 开门

Closed
guānmén 关门

💬 Language

Basics

Hello 你好 *Nǐhǎo*

Goodbye
再见 *Zàijiàn*

How are you?
你好吗？ *Nǐhǎo má?*

Fine 好 *Hǎo*

And you?
你呢？ *Nǐ ne?*

Please ... 请... *Qǐng ...*

Thank you
谢谢你 *Xièxiè nǐ*

Excuse me
劳驾 *Láojià*

Sorry.
对不起 *Duìbùqǐ*

Yes 是 *Shì*

No 不是 *Bùshì*

Mandarin Chinese – or Pǔtōnghuà (common speech), as it's referred to by the Chinese – can be written using the Roman alphabet. This system is known as Pinyin; in the following phrases we have provided both Mandarin script and Pinyin.

Mandarin has 'tonal' quality – the raising and lowering of pitch on certain syllables. There are four tones in Mandarin, plus a fifth 'neutral' tone that you can all but ignore. In Pinyin the tones are indicated with accent marks on vowels: **ā** (high), **á** (rising), **ǎ** (falling-rising), **à** (falling).

To enhance your trip with a phrasebook, visit **lonelyplanet.com**. Lonely Planet iPhone phrase-books are available through the Apple App store.

Do you speak English?
你会说英文吗？   *Nǐ huì shuō Yīngwén má?*

I don't understand.
我不明白.   *Wǒ bù míngbái.*

🚨 Emergencies

Help!	救命！	*Jiùmìng!*
Go away!	走开！	*Zǒukāi!*
Call a doctor!	请叫医生来!	*Qǐng jiào yīshēng lái!*
Call the police!	请叫警察!	*Qǐng jiào jǐngchá!*
I'm lost.	我迷路了.	*Wǒ mílù le.*
I'm sick.	我生病了.	*Wǒ shēngbìng le.*
Where are the toilets?	厕所在哪儿？	*Cèsuǒ zài nǎr?*

Numbers

一 *yī*   二/两 *èr/liǎng*   三 *sān*   四 *sì*   五 *wǔ*

✕ Eating & Drinking

I'd like ...
我要… Wǒ yào...

a table for two 一张两个人的桌子
yīzhāng liǎnggè rén de zhuōzi

the drink list 酒水单 jiǔshuǐ dān

the menu 菜单 càidān

a beer 啤酒 píjiǔ

a coffee 咖啡 kāfēi

I don't eat ...
我不吃… Wǒ bùchī...

fish 鱼 yú

poultry 家禽 jiāqín

red meat 牛羊肉 niúyángròu

SIGNS

Information
问讯处
Wènxùnchù

Entrance	入口	Rùkǒu
Exit	出口	Chūkǒu
Open	开	Kāi
Closed	关	Guān
Prohibited	禁止	Jìnzhǐ
Toilets	厕所	Cèsuǒ
Men	男	Nán
Women	女	Nǚ

--- **TIME & NUMBERS** ---

What time is it? 现在几点钟？ Xiànzài jǐdiǎn zhōng?
It's (10) o'clock. (十)点钟. (Shí)diǎn zhōng.
Half past (10). (十)点三十分. (Shí)diǎn sānshífēn.

morning	早上	zǎoshàng	**yesterday**	昨天	zuótiān
afternoon	下午	xiàwǔ	**today**	今天	jīntiān
evening	晚上	wǎnshàng	**tomorrow**	明天	míngtiān

🛍 Shopping

I'd like to buy...	我想买…	Wǒ xiǎng mǎi...
I'm just looking.	我先看看.	Wǒ xiān kànkàn.
How much is it?	多少钱？	Duōshǎo qián?
That's too expensive.	太贵了.	Tàiguì le.
Can you lower the price?	能便宜 一点吗？	Néng piànyí yīdiǎn má?

 6 六 liù

 7 七 qī

 8 八 bā

 9 九 jiǔ

 10 十 shí

Index

Sights p000   Map pages p000

Eating

Send Us Your Feedback

We love to hear from travellers – your comments help make our books better. We read every word, and we guarantee that your feedback goes straight to the authors. Visit lonelyplanet.com/contact to submit your updates and suggestions.

Note: We may edit, reproduce and incorporate your comments in Lonely Planet products such as guidebooks, websites and digital products, so let us know if you are happy to have your name acknowledged. For a copy of our privacy policy visit lonelyplanet.com/legal.

Acknowledgements

Cover photograph: The Temple of Heaven. cowardlion/Shutterstock ©

Back photograph: Walking the Great Wall at Badaling. Chintung Lee/Shutterstock ©

THIS BOOK

Destination Editor
Darren O'Connell

Cartographer
Julie Sheridan

Production Editor
Claire Rourke

Book Designer
Dermot Hegarty

Script Check
Piera Chen

Assisting Editors
Helen Koehne,
Kellie Langdon

Cover Researcher
Lauren Egan

Thanks to
Sofie Andersen, Imogen Bannister, Jessica Boland, Alison Killilea, Kate Mathews, Jennifer McDonagh

Although the authors and Lonely Planet have taken all reasonable care in preparing this book, we make no warranty about the accuracy or completeness of its content and, to the maximum extent permitted, disclaim all liability arising from its use.

Published by Lonely Planet Global Limited
CRN 554153
5th edition – Dec 2024
ISBN 978 1 78657 383 4
© Lonely Planet 2024
Photographs © as indicated 2024
10 9 8 7 6 5 4 3 2 1
Printed in Malaysia